# Table of Contents

## I. Introduction

- Importance of MS SQL in modern data management
- Purpose of the guide: empowering beginners to enhance their MS SQL skills
- Overview of what to expect from the guide

## II. Understanding MS SQL Basics

- Brief history and evolution of MS SQL
- Core concepts: databases, tables, rows, columns, SQL queries
- Introduction to Management Studio: interface and basic navigation

## III. Setting Up Your MS SQL Environment

- Installation process for MS SQL Server
- Configuring databases and security settings
- Connecting to databases using Management Studio

## IV. Essential SQL Commands and Syntax

- SELECT statement: retrieving data from tables
- INSERT, UPDATE, DELETE: manipulating data
- Filtering data with WHERE clause
- Sorting data with ORDER BY
- Joining tables: INNER JOIN, LEFT JOIN, RIGHT JOIN
- Grouping data with GROUP BY
- Introduction to subqueries

## V. Optimizing Database Performance

- Understanding indexes: types and usage
- Writing efficient queries
- Utilizing execution plans for query optimization
- Managing database statistics and fragmentation
- Techniques for improving query performance

## VI. Advanced SQL Concepts

- Stored procedures: creation and usage
- Triggers: automating actions based on database events
- Transactions: ensuring data integrity
- Common Table Expressions (CTEs) and window functions
- Handling exceptions and errors

## VII. Data Security and Maintenance

- Implementing user roles and permissions
- Backup and restore strategies
- Monitoring database health and performance
- Regular maintenance tasks: index rebuilds, statistics updates

## VIII. Integration with Other Technologies

- Connecting MS SQL with programming languages (e.g., Python, C#)
- Using MS SQL in web development (e.g., ASP.NET, PHP)
- Incorporating MS SQL in business intelligence solutions (e.g., Power BI)

## IX. Best Practices and Resources for Further Learning

- Tips for continuous improvement in MS SQL skills
- Recommended books, online courses, and communities
- Staying updated with MS SQL trends and advancements

## X. Conclusion

- Recap of key takeaways
- Encouragement for beginners to continue exploring and practicing
- Final thoughts and well wishes for their journey in mastering MS SQL.

# INTRODUCTION

In today's information-driven world, knowledge of database management systems is not only an important skill but also an essential one. Whether you are a data analyst, software developer or database administrator, knowledge of Microsoft SQL Server (MS SQL) can open the doors to many career opportunities and help you work efficiently and analyze big data. But for beginners, stepping into the world of MS SQL can seem daunting. The seemingly complex syntax, countless features, and technical details can be easy at first.

Don't worry because this e-book is your comprehensive guide to demystify MS SQL and start the journey of skill and knowledge development. Designed for beginners, this e-book will provide you with basic concepts, information and practical exercises to improve your MS SQL skills and solve problems.

## The Beginner's Advantage

First, let's address the elephant in the room: You are the one who started it. Perfect! In fact, being a beginner in the world of MS SQL has its own advantages. As a beginner, you have a fresh perspective, free from preconceived notions or ingrained habits. You have the opportunity to approach MS SQL with a curious mind, explore its complexities and unlock its potential.

## What to Expect

In this eBook, we'll embark on a step-by-step journey that will take you from MS SQL novice to proficient practitioner. Here's a sneak peek of what's in store:

Understanding MS SQL Basics: We will start with the basics and cover basic concepts such as databases, tables, SQL queries and the MS SQL Management Studio interface. By building a solid foundation, you'll have the confidence to easily transition to the MS SQL environment.

Setting Up Your MS SQL Environment: No journey can begin without proper planning. You will learn how to install MS SQL Server, configure a database, and create a secure connection using Management Studio. Once you've set up your site, you're ready to dive headfirst into the world of MS SQL.

Essential SQL Commands and Syntax: SQL is a database language and knowing its syntax is key to taking advantage of all the features of MS SQL. We will examine basic expressions such as SELECT, INSERT, UPDATE, DELETE and search techniques such as JOIN and subqueries. Thanks to examples and exercises, you will improve your SQL skills and learn to manage data correctly.

Optimizing Database Performance: Efficiency is important in database management. You'll find strategies to improve query performance, leverage indexes, and manage data state. By applying best practices, you will ensure that your MS SQL environment runs efficiently and effectively.

Advanced SQL Concepts: Once you're done, we'll dive into more advanced topics like stored procedures, triggers, transitions, and multiple instruction sets (CTEs). These techniques will help you work efficiently, improve data integrity, and solve complex analytical problems.

Data Security and Maintenance: Security cannot be compromised when processing sensitive information. You'll learn how to implement security measures, perform regular backups, and monitor data health to protect your important data.

## Your Journey Begins Here

Approach this path with an open mind and a desire to learn. Whether you're a student, a professional transitioning into a new role, or simply someone with a passion for data, this eBook is your gateway to mastering MS SQL. With the dedication, practice, and advice in these pages, you'll soon find yourself navigating the world of MS SQL with confidence and skill.

So, are you ready to unleash the power of MS SQL? Come on now and let's start this transformation journey together.

The Importance of MS SQL in Modern Data Management In today's digital age, information is at the forefront. From global organizations to small businesses, and from government agencies to nonprofits, the ability to manage and use data has become a critical part of business. In this context, Microsoft SQL Server (MS SQL) has become the foundation of modern data management, allowing organizations to store, retain and analyze data efficiently and accurately..

# The Evolution of Data Management

Before moving on to the basics of MS SQL, it is necessary to understand the evolution of database management. In the early days of computing, data was often stored in flat files or simple hierarchies. But as the volume and complexity of data grows exponentially, traditional data systems are proving inadequate to handle data growth.

The emergence of Relational Database Management Systems (RDBMS) has revolutionized information management by introducing the concept of organization. Data is organized into tables, columns and rows. This relational model underpins modern database systems by providing a flexible and extensible framework for storing and retrieving data.

# Enter MS SQL: A Brief Overview

Microsoft SQL Server, commonly referred to as MS SQL, is the leading RDBMS developed by Microsoft Corporation. Since its inception in the late 1980s, MS SQL has become a powerful and effective platform that meets most data management needs in businesses.

MS SQL provides a comprehensive set of tools and services for database management, business intelligence and data analysis. From small deployments to enterprise solutions, MS SQL scales seamlessly to meet the diverse needs of organizations of all sizes.

# The Role of MS SQL in Modern Data Management

## 1. Data Storage and Retrieval

At its core, MS SQL acts as a reliable and efficient source for storing and organizing data. Whether it is business data in e-commerce, customer data in a CRM system, or sensor data from IoT devices, MS SQL provides a process designed to store different information.

MS SQL's powerful indexing functionality accelerates data retrieval, allowing users to access the information they need quickly and effectively. Additionally, features such as partitioning and compression optimize storage usage, reduce costs and improve performance.

## 2. Data Security and Compliance

In an age where data privacy and regulatory requirements are becoming increasingly stringent, the security and integrity of your data is crucial. MS SQL provides a strong security system that includes access control, access and authentication to prevent unauthorized or compromised data.

Additionally, MS SQL enables organizations to implement business standards and regulatory requirements such as GDPR, HIPAA, and PCI DSS. Organizations can reduce the risk of data breaches and regulatory penalties by implementing stringent security measures and control methods.

## 3. Business Intelligence and Analytics

In addition to operating as a database, MS SQL allows organizations to gain insight from their data through advanced analytics and business intelligence (BI) capabilities. With tools like SQL Server Analysis Services (SSAS) and SQL Server Reporting Services (SSRS), organizations can perform multiple analyses, create interactive dashboards, and generate cutting-edge reports.

MS SQL also integrates with popular BI tools such as Power BI, allowing users to visualize and explore data in an intuitive and interactive way. MS SQL liberates access to data and insights, enabling organizations to increase business innovation, efficiency and profitability.

## 4. Scalability and Performance

As data volumes continue to grow, scalability and performance become important when it comes to data management. MS SQL is designed to scale seamlessly from single server deployments to multiple teams and distributed models.

With features such as database sharding, parallel query processing, and in-memory OLTP, MS SQL provides the performance and scalability needed to meet the most demanding needs. Whether you're processing millions of transactions per second or instantly analyzing petabytes of data, MS SQL has the power to meet today's needs.

## 5. Integration with Ecosystem

Integrates seamlessly with the broader Microsoft ecosystem, including MS SQL, Azure cloud services, .NET development and the Office productivity suite. This tight integration allows organizations to leverage existing Microsoft technologies and infrastructures while leveraging the power of MS SQL for database management and mining.

In addition, MS SQL supports interoperability with many third-party tools and applications. platform to ensure compatibility with different data and applications. Whether integrating with legacy systems, connecting to other sites, or using hybrid cloud solutions, MS SQL provides the flexibility and interoperability needed to meet the changing needs of today's companies.

In summary, MS SQL plays an important role in modern data management, becoming the basis of success in the data world. From storing and storing data to ensure security and compliance, to supporting business intelligence and analytics, to delivering scalability and performance, MS SQL provides comprehensive processes and capabilities to meet the diverse needs of organizations across industries.

With MS SQL skills, professionals can unlock new ways to improve performance, drive innovation in their organizations, and leverage the full potential of their data to achieve good goals. As we continue to face the challenges of the digital age, MS SQL remains a reliable partner in the search for data-driven insights and competitive advantage.

# Empowering Beginners to Enhance Their MS SQL Skills: The Purpose of This Guide

Microsoft SQL Server (MS SQL) proficiency is one of the best skills in the field of database administration. Whether you're a student looking to get into data analysis, a software developer looking to improve your skills, or a business professional looking to gain insight from your data organization, knowledge of MS SQL can open the door to many opportunities.

However, for beginners, mastering the intricacies of MS SQL can be a daunting task. There is a learning curve to overcome from understanding the basics of relational databases to writing SQL queries effectively. This is where this training comes into play.

## Understanding the Purpose

The main purpose of this guide is to help beginners improve their MS SQL skills. Whether you're entering the world of databases for the first time or looking to deepen your understanding of the basics of SQL, this guide is designed to give you the information, resources, and endorsements you need to succeed.

## Breaking Down the Barrier to Entry

One of the biggest problems beginners face when learning MS SQL is the amount of data. From information technology to online tutoring, the number of resources can be intimidating and confusing. This guide is designed to eliminate barriers to entry by presenting complex concepts in a clear, concise, and beginner-friendly way.

This guide makes it easy for beginners to understand and manage the learning process by presenting key concepts with simple and easy-to-understand explanations, instructions and examples. Whether you're a visual learner who loves graphics and illustrations or a hands-on learner who benefits from an interactive experience, you'll find materials and curriculum to suit your education..

## Building a Strong Foundation

This guide believes that a solid foundation is essential to mastering MS SQL. Just like a skyscraper needs a solid foundation to support its structure, the path to SQL knowledge begins with a good understanding of the basics. From database design to SQL syntax and query optimization techniques, this guide covers all the important topics you need to build a solid foundation in MS SQL.

By mastering the fundamentals, you'll gain the confidence and ability you need to tackle high-level concepts and real-world challenges with ease. Whether you're generating data, writing complex queries, or optimizing data, you'll have the knowledge and skills you need to succeed.

## Fostering a Growth Mindset

This guide is designed to provide knowledge and skills, as well as enhance the development of beginners. A growth mindset believes that skills and abilities can be developed through dedication and hard work. By adopting a growth mindset, beginners can approach learning with hope, patience, and perseverance in the face of challenges.

In this guide you will find encouragement, motivation and inspiration to keep you motivated to learn. Even if you encounter problems or obstacles along the way, remember that every challenge is an opportunity to learn and grow. With dedication, perseverance and determination, you will overcome all obstacles in your path and emerge stronger and wiser than ever before.

## Navigating Your Learning Journey

Learning MS SQL is not a one-size-fits-all endeavor. Everyone's learning is unique and there are many paths to success. Whether you are a self-directed individual who enjoys independent learning or someone who thrives on collaborative learning, this guide can give you the flexibility and freedom to customize your education to your own needs and interests.

You'll find a variety of resources and support networks to help you stay on track in your journey. Whether you're just getting started with MS SQL or moving towards mastering MS SQL, this guide is your guide to success.

In summary, the purpose of this guide is simple: to help beginners improve their MS SQL skills and begin a journey of learning, growth, and discovery. Whether you're a novice exploring the world of storage for the first time or an expert looking to improve your skills, this guide is your companion. Be confident every step of the way.

Providing you with the knowledge, help and support you need to succeed, this guide aims to demystify MS SQL and make learning as fun and rewarding as possible. what are you waiting for? Log in, explore and start traveling!

# Begin your journey to mastering MS SQL: Overview of what to expect from this guide

Welcome to your journey into Microsoft SQL Server (MS SQL) knowledge! Whether you're a newbie or have some database experience, this guide is designed to give you the information, tools, and resources you need to improve your MS SQL skills and effectively control and query your data.

## Understanding the Structure of the Guide

Before diving into the details of MS SQL, let's take some time to understand the structure of this guide. It is divided into several sections, each focusing on a different aspect of MS SQL. By following the progress of the topic, you will gradually improve your existing knowledge and understand MS SQL better from scratch.

## Part 1: Introduction to MS SQL

At the beginning of this guide, we will lay the foundations for you to step into the world of MS SQL. You will learn about the history and evolution of MS SQL, its importance in modern database management, and the countless possibilities it has for development and operations.

## Part 2: Getting Started with MS SQL

Once you understand the importance of MS SQL, we will move on to the practical part: Start with MS SQL. You will learn how to set up an MS SQL environment, install MS SQL Server, and configure databases using SQL Server Management Studio (SSMS). Once your environment is up and running, you're ready to dive into the basics of MS SQL.

## Part 3: Mastering SQL Fundamentals

After learning the basics, we will get to the heart of MS SQL: Structured Query Language (SQL). In this chapter, you'll learn the basics of SQL syntax, including querying data, filtering results, and performing simple data manipulation operations such as adding, modifying, and deleting records.

## Part 4: Advanced SQL Techniques

For your basic SQL knowledge, we will review the concepts and concepts in this section. You'll learn about joins, subqueries, and related expressions (CTEs), which are powe₹rful tools that enable you to extract insights from and manipulate complex data.

## Part 5: Optimizing Database Performance

In this chapter we shift our focus to database performance optimization - an essential part of MS SQL administration . You'll learn how to design a good database structure, create indexes to improve query performance, and optimize SQL queries for maximum performance.

## Part 6: Ensuring Data Security and Integrity

Security of information is important in today's digital environment. In this chapter, you will learn about the various security features and mechanisms built into MS SQL, including authentication, authorization, encryption, and auditing. You'll also find best practices for data integrity and regulatory compliance..

## Part 7: Integrating MS SQL with Other Technologies

MS SQL does not exist on its own; often needs to be combined with other technologies and systems. In this chapter, you will learn how to integrate MS SQL with programming languages such as Python and C#, web development frameworks such as ASP.NET and PHP, and business intelligence tools such as Power BI.

## Part 8: Best Practices and Further Learning

Finally, we will conclude this guide by discussing best practices for lifelong learning and professional development. In this tutorial, you'll find tips to help you stay up to date with the latest developments in MS SQL, recommended resources for further learning, and ideas to continue your journey to mastering MS SQL.

# Your Journey Begins Here

As we begin this journey together, please remember that mastering MS SQL is a marathon, not a race. It requires dedication, patience and a willingness to learn and improve. Whether you're a student, professional, or data enthusiast, this guide is your path to success in MS SQL.

So, without further ado, let's jump right in and begin our journey: Mastering MS SQL. Together we will explore the depths of relational data, uncover the mysteries of SQL syntax, and unlock the full capabilities of MS SQL for managing and analyzing data. Get ready for a fun adventure - start your MS SQL knowledge journey now!

# Unveiling the Evolution: A Brief History of MS SQL

In the world of database management, Microsoft SQL Server (MS SQL) is the foundation of innovation, reliability and performance. The journey of MS SQL, from its humble beginnings to its current position as the leading relational database management system (RDBMS), is a testament to technological advancement, the power of technology, and the growing need for information solutions.

## Origins: The Birth of MS SQL

The roots of MS SQL can be traced back to the late 1980s, when Microsoft recognized the need for a powerful database management system to complement its products. Microsoft collaborated with Sybase, one of the leading software companies of the time, to create a relational database management system called SQL Server.

In 1989, Microsoft SQL Server 1.0 was released, symbolizing the birth of SQL Server and becoming one of the most widely used systems in the world. Although its features and capabilities were limited compared to modern RDBMS solutions, SQL Server laid the foundation for future iterations and established Microsoft's position in the database business

## Evolution: Milestones and Innovations

MS SQL in the 1990s and early 2000s has undergone various changes. Significant evolution and expansion driven by technological advances and feedback from users and developers. Key features and innovations during this period include:

**1. SQL Server 4.2 (1993)**: SQL Server 4.2 provides support for client/server architecture and distributed business, and advances efficiency and effectiveness.

**2. SQL Server 6.5 (1996)**: With the release of SQL Server 6.5, Microsoft introduced many new features, including support for stored procedures, triggers, and OLAP (online analytical processing) functions. These improvements form the basis for SQL Server's emergence as a comprehensive database.

**3. SQL Server 7.0 (1998)**: SQL Server 7.0 represents an overhaul of the platform, introducing a new storage engine (Microsoft SQL Server Engine, or MSDE) and supporting database storage and database search. These features make SQL Server a solution for enterprise-level data management and analysis.

**4. SQL Server 2000 (2000)**: Building on the success of previous versions, SQL Server 2000 introduces new features such as XML support, advanced database analysis services, and increases scalability and performance. This release solidifies SQL Server's reputation as the leading RDBMS in the industry.

**5. SQL Server 2005 (2005)**: With the release of SQL Server 2005, Microsoft introduced many new features and improvements, including native support for the .NET programming language, database mirroring for high availability, and SQL Server Login to Management Studio (SSMS). introduced. ) tool. These innovations further strengthen SQL Server as a versatile and powerful database platform.

**6. SQL Server 2008 (2008)**: SQL Server 2008 brings many changes, including spatial data support, transparent data encryption and policy management. SQL Server 2008 R2 also introduces PowerPivot for Excel, allowing users to perform data analysis directly in Excel spreadsheets.

**7. SQL Server 2012 (2012)**: With the release of SQL Server 2012, Microsoft is committed to providing Excel with an effective platform for managing and analyzing structured and unstructured data. Key features introduced in SQL Server 2012 include AlwaysOn clustering to improve object availability, columnstore indexes to improve database performance, and SQL Server Tools for eight enhanced databases for ease of use.

**8. SQL Server 2014 (2014)**: SQL Server 2014 continues its tradition of innovation by introducing features such as in-memory OLTP to improve business performance, no expansion pools to optimize memory usage, and enhance disaster recovery from AlwaysOn Availability Groups.

**9. SQL Server 2016 (2016)**: With the release of SQL Server 2016, Microsoft is shifting its focus to cloud integration and advanced analytics. Key features introduced in SQL Server 2016 include native support for the JSON data format, improved integration with Azure cloud services, and the introduction of the R programming language for in-database analysis.

**10. SQL Server 2017 (2017)**: SQL Server 2017 marks a significant milestone in the evolution of the platform by introducing support for the Linux operating system, Docker containers, and image database capabilities. These improvements extend SQL Server's reach beyond the Windows ecosystem and position it as a truly competitive database platform.

**11. SQL Server 2019 (2019)**: SQL Server 2019, the latest version of SQL Server, is designed for leaders and delivers many achievements, including big data support, smart search and advanced security features. Moreover, SQL Server 2019 embraces the era of hybrid cloud computing, improves integration with Azure services and improves support for Kubernetes container orchestration.

# Impact: The Legacy of MS SQL

When we think about the evolution of MS SQL, its effect is far from clean. exceeded our expectations. Beyond data management. From critical role in business to enabling advanced analytics and machine learning, MS SQL has become an essential tool for organizations in various industries.

In addition, MS SQL's commitment to innovation, reliability and performance has earned the trust and confidence of millions of users worldwide. Whether you're an application developer, data analyst, or a DBA managing complex databases, MS SQL continues to help people and organizations unlock the potential of their data..

# Embracing the Future

As we complete our journey through the history of MS SQL, it is important to know that the evolution of the platform is not over yet. With each new release, Microsoft continues to push the boundaries of what's possible in data management and analysis, driving innovation and shaping the future of technology.

Whether you're a SQL veteran or just starting to explore the world of SQL, the legacy of MS SQL is the first repository of the changing power of technology to help people and organizations achieve their goals. As we embrace the future of MS SQL, let's continue to innovate, explore, and push the boundaries of what's possible in data management.

# Mastering the Core Concepts of MS SQL: A Comprehensive Guide for Beginners

In the broad landscape of database management, understanding the basics of Microsoft SQL Server (MS SQL) is crucial for anyone who wants to leverage the power of the relational database. Whether you are a data analyst, software developer, or database administrator, knowledge of these resources will enable you to succeed in MS SQL. In this section, we will examine the main elements that form the backbone of MS SQL, including files, tables, rows, columns and SQL queries.

## 1. Databases: The Foundation of MS SQL

At the heart of MS SQL lies the idea of a database, the process of collecting data to store, store and manage data effectively. Check. Think of a database as a digital warehouse where you can store and organize information. Each database in MS SQL is a separate container for related data, allowing you to manage and manage data accurately and effectively

## 2. Tables: Organizing Data into Structured Units

In data, information is organized into tables, which are two-dimensional models available. . lines and stripes. Think of the table as a virtual spreadsheet, where each row represents a specific data and each row represents a different feature or field. Tables work as building blocks of data, providing a structured way to store and organize data as needed..

### 3. Rows: Individual Records within a Table

A row, also called a tuple, represents a single record in the table. Each row in the table contains a combination of values corresponding to each row defined in the table schema. For example, in a table where employee data is stored, each row may represent a different employee; Rows can contain attributes such as name, age, and department. Rows work as atomic units of data in a table, allowing you to represent individuals and relationships in the database.

### 4. Columns: Attributes and Fields of Data

Columns, also called fields or attributes, represent individual data in a table. Each field is associated with a specific data type, such as number, string, date, or binary data, which determines the type of value that can be stored in the column. Columns define the structure and properties of data stored in a table, allowing you to control data integrity and perform precise analysis, filtering and indexing.

### 5. SQL Queries: Retrieving and Manipulating Data

Structured Query Language (SQL) is a language for relational databases and provides a standard syntax for interacting with and managing data. SQL queries allow you to retrieve, insert, update and delete data from tables, perform calculations and joins, and define relationships between tables. SQL queries consist of various elements, including expressions (such as SELECT, INSERT, UPDATE, DELETE), clauses (such as WHERE, GROUP BY, ORDER BY), and expressions (mathematical expressions such as math, string function). These terms apply to you. Ability to express complex logic and derive meaningful information from information.

## Putting It All Together: Practical Examples

To illustrate the main points in practice, let's take a good example: managing employee information in the company's database. We will create a table to store employee information with each row including employee ID, name, age, department, and salary. By using SQL queries, you will be able to do many things on the table and go to the world of MS SQL. Good And use the ability to manage and analyze data well, hoping to stand out in data management. By understanding the fundamentals of databases, tables, rows, columns, and SQL queries, you will gain the knowledge and skills needed to create and manage powerful solutions, perform complex data analysis tasks, and drive decisions in your organization. Whether you are a newcomer to the world of MS SQL or an expert looking to improve your skills, knowing these basic concepts will set you up for success in the changing and evolving world of information management.:

**Creating the Table**:

```
CREATE TABLE Employees
(EmployeeID INT, Name VARCHAR(50), Age INT, Department VARCHAR(50));`
```

**Inserting Data**:

```
INSERT INTO Employees VALUES (1, 'Sameer Gaikwad', 30, 'Marketing');
```

**Retrieving Data**:

```
SELECT * FROM Employees WHERE Department = 'Marketing';
```

**Updating Data**:

```
UPDATE Employees SET Age = 28 WHERE EmployeeID = 1;
```

**Deleting Data**:

```
DELETE FROM Employees WHERE EmployeeID = 1;
```

By mastering these core concepts and understanding how to use SQL queries to interact with data, you'll be well-equipped to navigate the world of MS SQL and leverage its capabilities to manage and analyze data effectively.

## Building a Strong Foundation for Success

In summary, knowing the basics of MS SQL is crucial for anyone who wants to succeed in the world of database management. By understanding the fundamentals of databases, tables, rows, columns, and SQL queries, you will gain the knowledge and skills needed to create and manage powerful solutions, perform complex data analysis tasks, and drive decisions in your organization. Whether you are a newcomer to the world of MS SQL or an expert looking to improve your skills, knowing these basic concepts will set you up for success in the changing and evolving world of information management.

## Mastering the Core Concepts of MS SQL: A Comprehensive Guide for Beginners

Microsoft SQL Server (MS SQL) is the foundation of efficiency, reliability and scalability in many data management environments. At the heart of MS SQL lie the fundamental concepts that form the basis of database management and querying. In this chapter, we will delve into these basic concepts (databases, tables, rows, columns, and SQL queries) to provide a better understanding of the building blocks of MS SQL.

## Understanding Databases:

In fact, data warehousing is the process of collecting necessary information for efficient access, management and storage. In the context of MS SQL, a database acts as a container for tables, views, stored procedures, and other database objects. Think of a database as a virtual warehouse where data is stored and managed.

**Key Points to Remember:**
- Databases provide a logical and physical structure for organizing data.
- MS SQL supports the creation of multiple databases within a single instance, allowing for segregation and management of different datasets.

## Exploring Tables:

Tables are the building blocks of databases in MS SQL. A table represents a two-dimensional structure consisting of columns and rows. Tables play an important role in organizing and organizing data in a relational database model.

**Key Points to Remember:**
- Tables consist of rows (records) and columns (fields).
- Each column in a table has a data type that defines the type of data it can store (e.g., integer, string, date).
- Primary keys are used to uniquely identify rows within a table, ensuring data integrity and enabling efficient data retrieval.

## Understanding Rows and Columns:

Rows and columns are methods of creating data in tables in MS SQL. Lines represent a single file or document, while rows represent specific fields or fields in that file. Rows and rows together form the structure of the table, allowing you to store, store and manage information in the design and layout.

**Key Points to Remember:**
- Rows contain the actual data stored within a table, with each row representing a single instance of the data entity.
- Columns define the attributes or properties of the data entity, specifying the type of data that can be stored in each field.
- Rows are sometimes referred to as records or tuples, while columns are also known as fields or attributes.

## Mastering SQL Queries:

SQL (Structured Query Language) is a language used to communicate with databases such as MS SQL. SQL queries allow you to store, manage and manipulate data stored in MS SQL databases. Whether you're retrieving data from a single table or performing complex data operations across multiple tables, SQL queries are the primary way to interact with your data.

**Key Points to Remember:**
- SQL queries consist of various components, including SELECT, FROM, WHERE, GROUP BY, HAVING, ORDER BY, and JOIN clauses.
- SELECT is used to specify the columns to retrieve from the database, while FROM specifies the tables from which to retrieve data.
- WHERE allows you to filter rows based on specific conditions, while GROUP BY enables you to group rows based on common values.
- HAVING filters group rows based on specified conditions, while ORDER BY sorts the resulting rows based on specified criteria.
- JOIN clauses allow you to combine data from multiple tables based on related columns, enabling you to perform complex data retrievals and manipulations.

# Putting It All Together:

We have now reviewed the following basic concepts: WE SQL databases, tables, rows, columns and SQL queries — let's put our new knowledge into practice. In the following sections of this guide, we provide examples and exercises designed to improve your MS SQL understanding and skills..

## Hands-On Exercises:

1. Create a new database in MS SQL Server Management Studio.
2. Define a table schema with appropriate columns and data types.
3. Insert sample data into the table using SQL INSERT statements.
4. Write SQL SELECT queries to retrieve specific data from the table.
5. Use SQL WHERE clause to filter rows based on specific criteria.
6. Perform basic data manipulations such as updating and deleting rows using SQL UPDATE and DELETE statements.
7. Practice using SQL JOINs to combine data from multiple tables in a single query.
8. Experiment with advanced SQL features such as subqueries, aggregations, and window functions to perform complex data analysis and manipulation.

In this section we introduce the main concepts of MS SQL (databases, tables, rows, columns and SQL queries). These core concepts are the building blocks of MS SQL and give you the foundation you need to master database administration and querying.

As you continue to learn MS SQL, remember to practice regularly, try different SQL queries and techniques, and don't hesitate to ask for help or guidance when necessary. With dedication, patience, and a deep understanding of the basic concepts, you will soon find yourself navigating the world of MS SQL with confidence and skill.

# Navigating MS SQL Management Studio: An Essential Introduction for Beginners

Microsoft SQL Server Management Studio (SSMS) is used as the primary interface for interacting with Microsoft SQL Server (MS SQL). As a beginner, knowledge of SSMS is required to effectively manage data, write SQL queries, and perform administrative tasks in the MS SQL environment. In this section, we will give a general introduction to SSMS, including its interface, easy-to-navigate features, and important tools for beginners.

## Understanding the Interface

When you first launch SQL Server Management Studio, you'll be greeted by a familiar interface consisting of several key components:

1. Menu Bar: The menu is located at the top of the SSMS window and provides access to various commands and options for managing data, running queries, and setting up SSMS. Here you'll find File, Edit, View, and Tools, each with commands and options.

2. Toolbar: Below the menu bar, you'll find the Toolbar, which contains a set of shortcut buttons for frequently used commands and actions. The toolbar provides quick access to functions such as opening new query windows, connecting to databases, and processing queries.

3. Object Explorer: The Object Explorer pane on the left side of the SSMS window serves as a central function for navigating and managing database objects. Here you can view and interact with databases, tables, views, stored procedures, and other objects in the SQL Server instance.

4. Query Editor: Query Editor is your central workspace for writing and executing SQL queries. It has a script window where you can enter SQL code and tabs for managing multiple query windows at once. Query Editor also provides features like keywords, short phrases, and IntelliSense to increase efficiency.

5. Results Pane: Below the query editor, you will see the results pane, which displays the results of the completed query in tabular form. Here you can view questions, check errors, and export data to various formats (such as Excel or CSV).

6. Status Bar: At the bottom of the SSMS window, you will see the status bar that provides information about the current status of SSMS, such as traffic status connection, execution and query execution time. The Status column also contains buttons to toggle through various options, such as the Details pane and Query Execution Plan..

## Basic Navigation Features

Now that we've familiarized ourselves with the SSMS interface, let's explore some basic navigation features to help you get started:

1. **Connecting to a Database**: To link to a file, click the Link button in the toolbar or choose Link from the menu. This will open the Connect to Server dialog where you can specify the server name, authentication method, and other connection details.

2. **Navigating Object Explorer**: Use the Object Explorer pane to navigate and interact with database objects. Expand nodes to view databases, tables, views, and other objects. You can create new files, run queries, and manage server locations directly from the Object Explorer.

3. **Opening Query Windows**: To open a new query window, click the New Query button in the toolbar or select New Query from the Menu. This will open a new tab in the Query Editor where you can enter and execute SQL queries.

4. **Executing Queries**: To complete the query, type or paste SQL code in the query editor window, then click the Done button on the toolbar or press F5. The query will be processed and the results will be displayed in the table below.

5. **Managing Query Tabs**: Manage multiple query windows simultaneously using tabs in the Query Editor. You can open new tabs, switch between tabs, and close tabs as needed. You can save the question script to disk or open an existing script directly from the question editor.

6. **Customizing SSMS**: SSMS has many options to customize the link to your liking. You can customize SSMS's appearance, adjust its size and color, and set keyboard shortcuts to make your projects work.

# Essential Tools for Beginners

As a beginner, there are several essential tools and features in SSMS that you'll want to familiarize yourself with:

**1. Object Explorer Details**: Use the Object Explorer Details pane to view detailed information about database objects, such as rows, indexes, and constraints. This pane provides an easy way to explore a document's template and understand its basic structure

**2. Template Explorer**: The Template Browser pane contains predefined SQL routines for many tasks and events, such as master tables, indexes, and stored procedures. You can use this template as a starting point for your own SQL scripts, saving time and effort during development.

**3. Activity Monitor**: The Performance Monitor tool provides quick information about the functionality and performance of your SQL statements. SQL Server execution example. You can use this tool to monitor resource usage, analyze long-running queries, and troubleshoot performance issues.

**4. Query Execution Plan**: The Query Execution Plan tool allows you to see the execution plan of a SQL query, helping you understand how the SQL Server engine executes and executes your query. This tool is useful for improving query performance and identifying potential bottlenecks in your code

**5. Registered Servers**: Use the name server feature to manage and configure connecting to multiple SQL Server instances through a single interface. You can group servers into folders, save connection credentials, and connect to your favorite servers easily and quickly.

# Mastering SSMS for Success

In conclusion, Microsoft SQL Server Management Studio (SSMS) serves as a gateway to Microsoft SQL Server (MS) for beginners and seasoned professionals alike. By mastering SSMS's interface, easy navigation features, and simple tools, you can manage data, write SQL queries, and perform administrative tasks with confidence and work well.

As you continue your journey using MS SQL, be sure to explore other functions and capabilities of SSMS, such as database management tools, data visualization tools, and integration with other Microsoft technologies. With practice, experience and a desire to learn, you will unlock the potential of SSMS and embed your ideas into the world of MS SQL.

# Mastering the Installation Process of MS SQL Server: A Beginner's Guide

Microsoft SQL Server (MS SQL) is a powerful relational database management system (RDBMS) that allows organizations to store, manage and analyze large amounts of data. Whether you are a data enthusiast, software developer, or IT professional, knowing the installation process of MS SQL Server is the first step in leveraging its capabilities. In this section, we provide a general guide to installing MS SQL Server, including various models, system requirements, configuration options, and beginner best practices.

# Understanding MS SQL Server Editions

Before diving into the installation process, it's important to understand the different editions of MS SQL Server available. Microsoft offers several editions of SQL Server, each tailored to specific use cases and licensing models:

**1. Express Edition**: Designed for developers and small businesses SQL Server Express is the free access edition of SQL Server. It provides simple storage functionality and is ideal for learning, development and small deployments.

**2. Developer Edition**: Similar to SQL Server Express, the developer edition is designed for developers and includes all the features of SQL Server Enterprise Edition. Licensed for development and testing purposes only, not for production use.

**3. Standard Edition**: SQL Server Standard Edition is a document suitable for most small and medium-sized businesses. High database capacity provides high capacity and supports business intelligence and data analysis.

**4. Enterprise Edition**: SQL Server Enterprise Edition is the most complete version of SQL Server; It offers powerful database performance, advanced security features and support for even more alarm operations. Suitable for large companies and organizations with stringent operational and scalability requirements

System Requirements

Before installing MS SQL Server, ensure that your system meets the minimum hardware and software requirements. The specific requirements may vary depending on the edition and version of SQL Server you're installing, but common prerequisites include:

**Operating System**:
Windows Server or Windows 10/11 Professional, Enterprise, or Education editions.

**Processor**:
Minimum 1.4 GHz 64-bit processor (2.0 GHz or faster recommended).

**Memory (RAM)**:
Minimum 1 GB (4 GB or more recommended).

**Disk Space**:
Minimum 6 GB of available hard disk space.

**.NET Framework**:
.NET Framework 4.6 or later.

Additionally, ensure that your system has the necessary permissions and prerequisites installed, such as administrative privileges, Windows PowerShell, and Visual C++ Redistributable Packages.

# Installation Options

MS SQL Server offers several installation options to suit different deployment scenarios and requirements. The two primary installation options are:

**1. Basic Installation**: Easy installation options provide an easy installation experience with minimal configuration options. It is suitable for beginners and users who want to quickly install SQL Server using the default environment. This option is ideal for development, testing and evaluation purposes.

**2. Custom Installation**: The installation option provides greater flexibility and control over the installation process. Instance settings allow you to customize various settings, such as selecting properties and configuring the database engine. This option is recommended for production facilities and advanced users that need specialized options.

# Step-by-Step Installation Guide

Now, let's walk through the step-by-step installation process for MS SQL Server:

1. Download the Installation Media: Visit the official Microsoft website or MSDN Subscriber Downloads to download the installation media for the desired edition and version of SQL Server.

2. Run the Installation Wizard: Double-click the downloaded setup file to launch the SQL Server Installation Center. Click on the "Installation" tab and select "New SQL Server stand-alone installation or add features to an existing installation."

3. Enter Product Key: Enter the product key or select the "Evaluation" edition if you're installing a trial version of SQL Server. Click "Next" to continue.

4. Accept License Terms: Read and accept the Microsoft Software License Terms. Click "Next" to proceed.

5. Install Setup Files: The installation wizard will check for prerequisites and install the necessary setup files. Once completed, click "Next" to continue.

6. Feature Selection: Select the features you want to install, such as Database Engine Services, Analysis Services, Reporting Services, and Management Tools. Click "Next" to proceed.

7. Instance Configuration: Specify the instance name and instance root directory. You can choose between a default instance or a named instance. Click "Next" to continue.

8. Server Configuration: Configure the SQL Server services, including the SQL Server Database Engine, SQL Server Agent, and SQL Server Browser. Specify the service accounts and authentication mode (Windows Authentication or Mixed Mode). Click "Next" to proceed.

9. Database Engine Configuration: Configure the authentication mode and specify the SQL Server administrators (sysadmins). You can also enable features such as Data Directories, TempDB configuration, and FILESTREAM. Click "Next" to continue.

10. Analysis Services Configuration: Configure the Analysis Services instance, if applicable. Specify the server mode (Multidimensional or Tabular) and authentication mode. Click "Next" to continue.

11. Reporting Services Configuration: Configure the Reporting Services instance, if applicable. Specify the installation mode (Native or SharePoint) and web service URL. Click "Next" to continue.

12. Ready to Install: Review the installation summary and verify the configuration settings. Click "Install" to begin the installation process.

13. Installation Progress: The installation wizard will now install SQL Server and configure the selected features. This process may take several minutes to complete.

14. Completion: Once the installation is complete, you'll see a confirmation message indicating that SQL Server was installed successfully. Click "Close" to exit the installation wizard.

# Post-Installation Tasks

After installing MS SQL Server, there are several post-installation tasks you may need to perform, including:

**Configuration**:
Configure additional settings such as memory allocation, security policies, and backup preferences.

**Security**:
Implement security best practices, such as creating strong passwords, limiting access permissions, and enabling encryption.

**Maintenance**:
Set up regular maintenance tasks such as database backups, index maintenance, and performance monitoring.

**Testing**:
Validate the installation and verify that SQL Server is functioning correctly by connecting to databases, executing queries, and performing basic operations.

# Unlocking the Power of MS SQL Server

Unleash the potential of MS SQL Server to streamline information administration, boost execution, and drive experiences. Tackle progressed highlights for productive capacity, lightning-fast inquiries, and consistent integration. Optimize database organization with strong security measures and robotized errands. Enable decision-making through real-time analytics and adaptable arrangements. Whether overseeing small-scale ventures or enterprise-level frameworks, MS SQL Server engages businesses with unparalleled unwavering quality and adaptability, moving them towards victory within the advanced age.

# Configuring Databases and Security Settings in MS SQL Server: A Beginner's Guide

In a dynamic data management environment, configuring databases and creating a secure environment is a must for every Microsoft SQL Server (MS SQL) administrator, leader or producer. Understanding how to create and manage data and implementing security measures to protect sensitive data is crucial to ensuring the integrity, availability, and confidentiality of this data in the MS SQL environment. In this chapter, we will provide an overview of database configuration and security in MS SQL Server, enabling beginners to understand the basic concepts of database management with confidence and wisdom.

# Configuring Databases

## Creating a Database

The first step in configuring a database in MS SQL Server is creating a new database. To create a database, follow these steps:

**1. Launch SQL Server Management Studio (SSMS)**: Open SSMS and connect to your SQL Server instance using appropriate credentials.

**2. Navigate to Object Explorer**: In Object Explorer, expand the server node, right-click on the "Databases" node, and select "New Database."

**3. Enter Database Name**: In the New Database dialog, enter a name for your database and configure additional settings such as filegroup allocation and file size.

**4. Configure Options**: Specify additional configuration options such as file locations, growth settings, and collation settings as needed.

**5. Click OK**: Once you've configured the database settings, click OK to create the database.

## Modifying Database Properties

After creating a database, you may need to modify its properties to meet specific requirements or optimize performance. To modify database properties, follow these steps:

1. **Right-click on Database**: In Object Explorer, right-click on the database you want to modify and select "Properties."

2. **Navigate to Options**: In the Database Properties dialog, navigate to the "Options" page to modify settings such as recovery model, compatibility level, and auto close.

3. **Modify Other Properties**: Explore other pages in the Database Properties dialog to modify additional settings such as file and filegroup properties, extended properties, and database options.

4. **Click OK**: Once you've made the necessary modifications, click OK to apply the changes to the database.

# Implementing Security Settings

## Authentication Modes

MS SQL Server supports two authentication modes: Windows Authentication and Mixed Mode Authentication (Windows Authentication and SQL Server Authentication). To configure authentication modes, follow these steps:

1. **Launch SSMS**: Open SSMS and connect to your SQL Server instance.

2. **Right-click on Server**: In Object Explorer, right-click on the server node and select "Properties."

3. **Navigate to Security Page**: In the Server Properties dialog, navigate to the "Security" page to configure authentication modes.

4. **Select Authentication Mode**: Choose either "Windows Authentication Mode" or "Mixed Mode Authentication" and click OK to apply the changes.

# Creating Logins and Users

Logins and users are principal entities used to grant access to SQL Server instances and databases, respectively. To create logins and users, follow these steps:

**1. Navigate to Security Folder**: In Object Explorer, expand the Security folder, right-click on the "Logins" node, and select "New Login" to create a new login.

**2. Enter Login Details**: In the New Login dialog, enter the login name, select authentication type (Windows or SQL Server), and configure login properties such as default database and server roles.

**3. Create User in Database**: To create a user in a specific database, right-click on the database, select "New User," and specify the user name and associated login.

**4. Assign Permissions**: After creating the user, assign appropriate permissions to the user within the database by granting or denying permissions on specific database objects.

# Configuring Database Roles

Database roles are groups of users with common sets of permissions within a database. To configure database roles, follow these steps:

**1. Navigate to Database Roles**: In Object Explorer, expand the database, and navigate to the "Security" folder. Right-click on "Database Roles" and select "New Database Role" to create a new role.

**2. Enter Role Name**: In the New Database Role dialog, enter a name for the role and specify its owner.

**3. Assign Permissions**: After creating the role, assign appropriate permissions to the role by granting or denying permissions on specific database objects.

**4. Add Members**: Add users to the role by selecting the role, navigating to the "Members" page, and adding users or other roles as members of the role.

# Strengthening Your Database Management Skills

In summary, setting up databases and creating security settings are simple tasks for any MS SQL Server administrator or developer. By understanding how to create and manage data, set authentication methods, create logins, users and permissions, you will be able to create honesty, security and confidentiality of your data in the MS SQL environment. Whether you're new to the world of data management or a seasoned professional looking to improve your skills, knowing these basic skills is crucial to success in effective and flexible information management. Through practice, experimentation, and a commitment to continuous learning, you will improve your data management skills and create new opportunities for growth and success in your career.

# Mastering Database Connections in Microsoft SQL Server Management Studio (SSMS)

## A Comprehensive Guide for Beginners

Mastering database connections in Microsoft SQL Server Management Studio (SSMS) is crucial for effective database management. SSMS provides many tools and features to make this task easier. First of all, it is easy to understand how to create a connection to the database. This includes entering the name server, authentication method (Windows or SQL Server), and certificate. Once connected, users can explore files using Object Explorer, which provides server objects (databases, tables, stored procedures, etc.). SSMS also allows multiple connections to be created and managed simultaneously, allowing users to access files at the same time. allows it to work with multiple databases or servers.Also, it is important to know the question window. SSMS provides a powerful query engine with critical content visualization, IntelliSense, and debugging features for effective querying. and notes.

Also SSMS includes Performance Monitor for monitoring server activity, Database Engine Optimization Advisor for performance, etc. It also provides features such as. Features, Exploring, mastering data connections in SSMS include knowing how to create connections, navigate data, make good use of the query window, and re-optimize SSMS general tools and features for effective data management.

# Chapter 1: Understanding Database Connections

## 1.1 Overview of Database Connections:

- Definition of database connections.
- Importance of establishing connections for database management tasks.
- Different types of connections supported by SSMS (Windows Authentication, SQL Server Authentication, Azure Active Directory Authentication, etc.).

## 1.2 Connection Options in SSMS:

- Exploring the various options available for establishing connections in SSMS.
- Configuring connection properties such as server name, authentication method, and database selection.
- Understanding advanced connection options and settings.

## 1.3 Connection Security:

- Importance of securing database connections to protect sensitive data.
- Best practices for ensuring secure connections in SSMS.
- Overview of encryption, SSL/TLS, and other security features for database connections.

# Chapter 2: Connecting to SQL Server Instances

## 2.1 Connecting to Local Instances:

- Step-by-step guide to connecting to SQL Server instances installed on the local machine.
- Configuring authentication methods and other connection settings.
- Troubleshooting common connection issues for local instances.

## 2.2 Connecting to Remote Instances:

- Establishing connections to SQL Server instances hosted on remote servers.
- Understanding network configurations, firewalls, and port settings for remote connections.
- Tips for securely connecting to remote instances over the internet.

## 2.3 Connecting to Named Instances:

- Differentiating between default and named instances of SQL Server.
- How to connect to named instances using SSMS.
- Specifying instance names and connection parameters for named instances.

# Chapter 3: Authentication Methods in SSMS

## 3.1 Windows Authentication:

- Overview of Windows Authentication and its benefits.
- Steps for connecting to SQL Server using Windows Authentication in SSMS.
- Considerations for domain-joined and non-domain-joined environments.

## 3.2 SQL Server Authentication:

- Understanding SQL Server Authentication and its use cases.
- Configuring SQL Server logins and passwords.
- Connecting to SQL Server using SQL Server Authentication in SSMS.

## 3.3 Azure Active Directory Authentication:

- Introduction to Azure Active Directory Authentication for SQL Server.
- Connecting to Azure SQL Database using Azure AD Authentication.
- Configuring Azure AD logins and permissions in SSMS.

# Chapter 4: Advanced Connection Scenarios

## 4.1 Connecting to Azure SQL Database:

- Overview of Azure SQL Database and its benefits.
- Establishing connections to Azure SQL Database from SSMS.
- Considerations for firewall rules, access control, and security in Azure.

## 4.2 Connecting to SQL Server on Linux:

- Exploring the support for SQL Server on Linux.
- Connecting to SQL Server instances running on Linux using SSMS.
- Configuration considerations and compatibility issues.

## 4.3 Connecting to SQL Server Failover Cluster Instances:

- Understanding failover clustering and its role in high availability.
- Establishing connections to SQL Server failover cluster instances.
- Failover scenarios and considerations for managing connections.

# Chapter 5: Managing and Organizing Connections

## 5.1 Saving and Managing Connection Profiles:

- How to save connection profiles for quick access in SSMS.
- Organizing connection profiles into folders and categories.
- Tips for managing and maintaining connection profiles effectively.

## 5.2 Configuring Connection Properties:

- Customizing connection properties and settings in SSMS.
- Adjusting timeout settings, packet sizes, and other connection parameters.
- Fine-tuning connection options for optimal performance and reliability.

## 5.3 Connection Pooling:

- Understanding connection pooling and its role in improving performance.
- Configuring connection pooling settings in SSMS.
- Monitoring and troubleshooting connection pooling issues.

# Chapter 6: Troubleshooting Connection Issues

## 6.1 Common Connection Errors:

- Overview of common errors encountered when establishing connections.
- Identifying error codes and messages in SSMS.
- Troubleshooting tips and techniques for resolving connection errors.

## 6.2 Network and Firewall Issues:

- Understanding network configurations and firewall settings.
- Troubleshooting connectivity issues related to network restrictions.
- Configuring firewall rules and port forwarding for SQL Server.

## 6.3 Security and Authentication Problems:

- Addressing security-related issues such as authentication failures.
- Troubleshooting permissions, logins, and access control settings.
- Best practices for securing connections and preventing unauthorized access.

# Mastering Database Connections in SSMS

As a result, mastering database cabling in Microsoft SQL Server Management Studio (SSMS) is important for someone working with MS SQL databases. By understanding various connections, authentication methods, and advanced scenarios, beginners can create secure and reliable connections to SQL Server instances, local or remote, on-premises or in the cloud. With the knowledge and skills gained in this comprehensive guide, beginners can lay the foundations for success in the world of MS SQL by exploring complex data connections with confidence and skill.

# Mastering the SELECT Statement: Retrieving Data from Tables in MS SQL Server

The SELECT statement is fundamental in retrieving data from tables in Microsoft SQL Server. It allows users to specify the data they want to retrieve and from which tables. The basic syntax of a SELECT statement includes the SELECT keyword followed by a list of columns or expressions to retrieve, and the FROM keyword followed by the table name. For example:

```
SELECT column1, column2 FROM TableName;
```

You can also use wildcard characters like '*' to select all columns:

```
SELECT * FROM TableName;
```

Additionally, you can filter data using the WHERE clause:

```
SELECT column1, column2 FROM TableName WHERE condition;
```

Moreover, you can perform calculations or manipulate data using functions within the SELECT statement. For instance:

```
SELECT column1, column2, column1 + column2 AS Sum FROM TableName;
```

The SELECT statement is versatile and can be extended with other clauses like ORDER BY, GROUP BY, HAVING, and JOIN to further refine and manipulate the retrieved data. Understanding and mastering the SELECT statement is crucial for effective data retrieval and manipulation in MS SQL Server.

# Chapter 1: Understanding the Basics of the SELECT Statement

## 1.1 Introduction to the SELECT Statement:

- Definition and purpose of the SELECT statement in MS SQL.
- Overview of the SELECT statement's role in querying and retrieving data from tables.

## 1.2 Syntax of the SELECT Statement:

- Exploring the syntax components of the SELECT statement, including SELECT clause, FROM clause, WHERE clause, and optional clauses such as ORDER BY, GROUP BY, and HAVING.
- Understanding the structure and sequence of the SELECT statement for constructing queries.

## 1.3 Retrieving All Columns vs. Specific Columns:

- Differentiating between selecting all columns (*) and selecting specific columns in the SELECT statement.
- Pros and cons of each approach and best practices for selecting columns based on requirements.

# Chapter 2: Filtering Data with the WHERE Clause

## 2.1 Introduction to the WHERE Clause:

- Role of the WHERE clause in filtering rows based on specified conditions.
- Overview of comparison operators, logical operators, and wildcard characters used in WHERE clause conditions.

## 2.2 Using Comparison Operators:

- Exploring the usage of comparison operators such as =, <>, <, >, <=, and >= in WHERE clause conditions.
- Examples illustrating how to filter data based on equality, inequality, and range conditions.

## 2.3 Applying Logical Operators:

- Understanding logical operators such as AND, OR, and NOT for combining multiple conditions in WHERE clause expressions.
- Guidelines for constructing complex WHERE clause conditions using logical operators.

# Chapter 3: Sorting Data with the ORDER BY Clause

## 3.1 Introduction to the ORDER BY Clause:

- Role of the ORDER BY clause in sorting query results based on specified columns.
- Overview of ascending (ASC) and descending (DESC) sorting options.

## 3.2 Sorting by Single Column:

- Examples demonstrating how to sort query results by a single column using the ORDER BY clause.
- Considerations for sorting text, numeric, date, and datetime columns.

## 3.3 Sorting by Multiple Columns:

- Exploring scenarios where sorting by multiple columns is required for achieving desired result ordering.
- Syntax and usage of the ORDER BY clause for sorting query results by multiple columns.

# Chapter 4: Grouping Data with the GROUP BY Clause

## 4.1 Introduction to the GROUP BY Clause:

- Role of the GROUP BY clause in grouping query results based on specified columns.
- Overview of aggregate functions and their usage in conjunction with GROUP BY clause.

## 4.2 Aggregating Data with Aggregate Functions:

- Understanding aggregate functions such as COUNT, SUM, AVG, MIN, and MAX for summarizing data within groups.
- Examples illustrating how to use aggregate functions in SELECT statements with GROUP BY clause.

## 4.3 Filtering Grouped Data with the HAVING Clause:

- Introduction to the HAVING clause for filtering grouped data based on aggregate function results.
- Syntax and usage of the HAVING clause in conjunction with GROUP BY clause.

# Chapter 5: Advanced Techniques and Best Practices

## 5.1 Subqueries:

- Introduction to subqueries and their role in nested SELECT statements.
- Examples demonstrating how to use subqueries for filtering, sorting, and aggregating data.

## 5.2 Joins:

- Overview of different types of joins (INNER JOIN, LEFT JOIN, RIGHT JOIN, FULL JOIN) for combining data from multiple tables.
- Syntax and usage of join clauses in SELECT statements.

## 5.3 Common Table Expressions (CTEs):

- Introduction to Common Table Expressions (CTEs) and their benefits for organizing and simplifying complex queries.
- Examples illustrating how to define and use CTEs in SELECT statements.

# Chapter 6: Optimizing Query Performance

## 6.1 Indexing:

- Understanding the role of indexes in optimizing query performance.
- Guidelines for creating, maintaining, and utilizing indexes for efficient data retrieval.

## 6.2 Query Execution Plan:

- Introduction to query execution plans and their importance in understanding how queries are processed and executed.
- Techniques for analyzing query execution plans and identifying performance bottlenecks.

## 6.3 Query Tuning:

- Strategies and best practices for tuning SELECT statements to improve query performance.
- Tools and utilities for monitoring and optimizing query execution in MS SQL Server.

# Mastering the Art of Data Retrieval with the SELECT Statement

As a result, knowledge of the SELECT statement is very important for anyone working with MS SQL Server databases. By understanding its syntax, functions, and best practices, beginners can create efficient and effective queries to retrieve data from tables accurately and precisely. With the knowledge and skills gained in this comprehensive guide, beginners can confidently solve data recovery problems in MS SQL Server, unlock new insights and technologies, and use data to drive decisions and achieve business goals.

# Mastering Data Manipulation: INSERT, UPDATE, DELETE in MS SQL Server

In Microsoft SQL Server, mastering data manipulation involves understanding and effectively utilizing the INSERT, UPDATE, and DELETE statements.

The **INSERT** statement is used to add new records into a table. It requires specifying the table name and the values to be inserted into each column. Optionally, you can specify the columns explicitly if you're not inserting values into all columns.

The **UPDATE** statement is used to modify existing records in a table. It requires specifying the table name, the columns to be updated, and the new values. Additionally, you can include a WHERE clause to filter which records to update based on specific conditions.

The **DELETE** statement is used to remove records from a table. Like the UPDATE statement, it requires specifying the table name and can also include a WHERE clause to specify which records to delete based on certain conditions.

It's crucial to exercise caution when using these statements, especially DELETE, as they directly affect the data in your database. Always ensure you have appropriate backup procedures in place and thoroughly test your statements before executing them in a production environment. Understanding the syntax and behavior of these statements is essential for effectively managing and manipulating data in Microsoft SQL Server.

# Chapter 1: Understanding Data Manipulation Operations

## 1.1 Introduction to Data Manipulation:

- Definition and importance of data manipulation operations in database management.
- Overview of INSERT, UPDATE, and DELETE statements and their roles in modifying data.

## 1.2 Data Modification Languages (DML):

- Introduction to Data Manipulation Language (DML) and its significance in SQL.
- Differentiating between DML and Data Definition Language (DDL) operations.

## 1.3 Transactions and Data Consistency:

- Understanding the concept of transactions and their impact on data consistency.
- Importance of transaction management in ensuring data integrity during data manipulation operations.

# Chapter 2: Inserting Data with the INSERT Statement

## 2.1 Syntax and Usage of the INSERT Statement:

- Exploring the syntax of the INSERT statement for adding new rows to a table.
- Overview of different INSERT statement variations, including single-row and multi-row inserts.

## 2.2 Inserting Data into Specific Columns:

- Techniques for specifying values for specific columns when inserting data.
- Examples illustrating how to insert data into tables with identity columns or computed columns.

## 2.3 Bulk Inserts and Performance Considerations:

- Introduction to bulk insert operations for efficiently adding large volumes of data.
- Best practices for optimizing performance during bulk insert operations.

# Chapter 3: Updating Data with the UPDATE Statement

## 3.1 Syntax and Usage of the UPDATE Statement:

- Exploring the syntax of the UPDATE statement for modifying existing data in a table.
- Overview of UPDATE statement components, including SET clause and WHERE clause.

## 3.2 Updating Data Based on Conditions:

- Techniques for specifying conditions to selectively update rows in a table.
- Examples demonstrating how to use logical and comparison operators in UPDATE statements.

## 3.3 Updating Data Using Joins:

- Leveraging JOIN operations to update data across multiple tables.
- Guidelines for using INNER JOIN, LEFT JOIN, and other join types in UPDATE statements.


# Chapter 4: Deleting Data with the DELETE Statement

## 4.1 Syntax and Usage of the DELETE Statement:

- Exploring the syntax of the DELETE statement for removing rows from a table.
- Overview of DELETE statement components, including WHERE clause for specifying deletion conditions.

## 4.2 Deleting Data Based on Conditions:

- Techniques for selectively deleting rows based on specified conditions.
- Examples illustrating how to use logical and comparison operators in DELETE statements.

## 4.3 Deleting Data Safely and Efficiently:

- Best practices for performing safe and efficient deletion operations.
- Considerations for managing cascading deletes, transactional consistency, and data recovery.

# Chapter 5: Transaction Management and Error Handling

## 5.1 Understanding Transactions:

- Introduction to transactions and their role in ensuring data consistency.
- Overview of transaction properties such as Atomicity, Consistency, Isolation, and Durability (ACID).

## 5.2 Transaction Control Statements:

- Exploring transaction control statements such as COMMIT, ROLLBACK, and SAVEPOINT.
- Techniques for managing transaction boundaries and handling transaction errors.

# Chapter 6: Advanced Data Manipulation Techniques

## 6.1 Using MERGE Statement for Upserts:

- Introduction to the MERGE statement for performing "upserts" (INSERT or UPDATE) based on specified conditions.
- Syntax and usage of the MERGE statement for handling data synchronization scenarios.

## 6.2 Performing Batch Updates and Deletes:

- Techniques for optimizing performance during batch update and delete operations.
- Strategies for processing large datasets efficiently while minimizing resource utilization.

## 6.3 Data Manipulation with Common Table Expressions (CTEs):

- Leveraging Common Table Expressions (CTEs) for complex data manipulation tasks.
- Examples demonstrating how to use CTEs in conjunction with INSERT, UPDATE, and DELETE statements.

# Chapter 7: Best Practices and Performance Optimization

## 7.1 Best Practices for Data Manipulation:

- Guidelines for writing efficient and maintainable INSERT, UPDATE, and DELETE statements.
- Considerations for data integrity, transaction management, and error handling.

## 7.2 Performance Optimization Techniques:

- Strategies for optimizing performance during data manipulation operations.
- Indexing, query tuning, and other optimization techniques for enhancing data manipulation performance.

## 7.3 Monitoring and Troubleshooting Data Manipulation:

- Tools and utilities for monitoring data manipulation activity in MS SQL Server.
- Techniques for troubleshooting common issues and performance bottlenecks.

# Mastering Data Manipulation in MS SQL Server

In summary, knowledge of database administration in MS SQL Server is crucial for anyone working with databases. By understanding the intricacies of INSERT, UPDATE, and DELETE statements, beginners can effectively update data, maintain data integrity, and drive business processes. With the knowledge and ideas gained in this comprehensive guide, beginners can confidently manage data in MS SQL Server and create new possibilities of using data to achieve the organization's goals.

# Mastering Data Filtering with the WHERE Clause in MS SQL Server

In the world of data management, the ability to filter and preserve unique data is critical to extracting understandable content and supporting trends. Expressions are powerful tools for filtering data based on specified criteria in Microsoft SQL Server (MS SQL), allowing users to narrow down queries and focus on data. In this guide, we will examine the intricacies of data filtering in MS SQL Server using the WHERE clause. Whether you're a novice exploring the basics of SQL or an expert looking to improve your querying skills, this guide will provide you with the knowledge and techniques you need to manage a database using MS SQL Server

# Chapter 1: Understanding the WHERE Clause

## 1.1 Introduction to the WHERE Clause:

- Definition and purpose of the WHERE clause in SQL queries.
- Overview of its role in filtering rows based on specified conditions.

## 1.2 Syntax of the WHERE Clause:

- Exploring the syntax components of the WHERE clause, including comparison operators, logical operators, and expressions.
- Understanding the structure and sequence of the WHERE clause in SQL queries.

## 1.3 Filtering Conditions:

- Understanding the different types of filtering conditions supported by the WHERE clause, such as equality, inequality, range, and pattern matching.
- Exploring the usage of comparison operators (=, <>, <, >, <=, >=) and logical operators (AND, OR, NOT) in filtering conditions.

# Chapter 2: Basic Filtering Techniques

## 2.1 Filtering by Single Condition:

- Techniques for filtering data based on a single condition using the WHERE clause.
- Examples illustrating how to filter rows based on equality, inequality, and range conditions.

## 2.2 Combining Multiple Conditions:

- Strategies for combining multiple filtering conditions using logical operators (AND, OR, NOT).
- Guidelines for constructing complex filtering expressions to meet specific criteria.

## 2.3 Using Parentheses for Precedence:

- Understanding the importance of parentheses for controlling the order of operations in complex filtering expressions.
- Examples demonstrating how to use parentheses to clarify the logic of filtering conditions.

# Chapter 3: Advanced Filtering Techniques

## 3.1 Filtering with Wildcard Characters:

- Introduction to wildcard characters (%) for pattern matching in filtering conditions.
- Techniques for using wildcard characters to match patterns within string data.

## 3.2 Filtering with NULL Values:

- Understanding how NULL values are handled in filtering conditions.
- Techniques for filtering rows with NULL values using IS NULL and IS NOT NULL predicates.

## 3.3 Filtering with Subqueries:

- Leveraging subqueries within the WHERE clause for advanced filtering scenarios.
- Examples demonstrating how to use subqueries to filter data based on results from other queries.


# Chapter 4: Filtering Techniques for Different Data Types

## 4.1 Filtering Numeric Data:

- Techniques for filtering numeric data types (integer, decimal, float) using comparison operators.
- Considerations for handling precision, rounding, and arithmetic operations in filtering conditions.

## 4.2 Filtering Textual Data:

- Strategies for filtering textual data types (varchar, char, text) using equality, inequality, and pattern matching operators.
- Techniques for case-insensitive filtering and handling collation settings.

## 4.3 Filtering Date and Time Data:

- Techniques for filtering date and time data types (datetime, date, time) using comparison operators and date functions.
- Examples illustrating how to filter data based on specific date ranges, intervals, and relative dates.

# Chapter 5: Performance Optimization and Indexing

## 5.1 Optimizing Filtering Performance:

- Strategies for optimizing query performance when using the WHERE clause for data filtering.
- Techniques for minimizing the number of rows scanned and maximizing query execution efficiency.

## 5.2 Indexing for Filtering Operations:

- Understanding the role of indexes in optimizing filtering operations.
- Guidelines for creating and maintaining indexes to improve query performance for filtering conditions.

# Chapter 6: Best Practices and Common Pitfalls

## 6.1 Best Practices for Data Filtering:

- Best practices for writing efficient and effective filtering conditions in SQL queries.
- Considerations for code readability, maintainability, and performance optimization.

## 6.2 Avoiding Common Pitfalls:

- Identification and avoidance of common pitfalls and errors when using the WHERE clause for data filtering.
- Techniques for troubleshooting and debugging filtering conditions.

# Chapter 7: Real-World Applications and Examples

## 7.1 Filtering Data in Practical Scenarios:

- Real-world examples and case studies demonstrating the application of filtering techniques in various scenarios.
- Use cases from different industries and domains showcasing the versatility of the WHERE clause in data analysis and decision-making.

# Mastering Data Filtering with the WHERE Clause

In summary, mastering the data filtering used is crucial for anyone working with SQL queries in MS SQL Server. By understanding its syntax, functionality, and best practices, beginners can effectively narrow down queries and extract relevant information from the database. With the knowledge and ideas gained in this comprehensive guide, beginners can confidently use filter techniques to query data in MS SQL Server, opening up new possibilities for analyzing data, reporting, and making decisions.

# Mastering Data Sorting with ORDER BY Clause in MS SQL Server

In MS SQL Server, the ORDER BY clause is pivotal for sorting query results in ascending or descending order based on specified columns. Its syntax is straightforward:

SELECT column1, column2, FROM table_name

ORDER BY column1 [ASC | DESC], column2 [ASC | DESC], ...

Here, column1, column2, etc., represent the columns by which you want to sort the result set. ASC (ascending) is the default sorting order, while DESC (descending) sorts the data in descending order.

Additionally, you can sort results using column aliases, expressions, or even ordinal positions. However, be cautious with ordinal positions as they might lead to ambiguous code and hinder readability.

It's worth noting that ORDER BY can impact query performance, especially on large datasets. To enhance performance, consider indexing columns involved in sorting operations.

Moreover, ORDER BY can be combined with other clauses like TOP, OFFSET, and FETCH to implement pagination or retrieve a specific number of rows.

Understanding the nuances of the ORDER BY clause empowers SQL developers to efficiently organize query results, thus improving the usability and performance of their database applications.

# Chapter 1: Understanding the ORDER BY Clause

## 1.1 Introduction to Sorting Data:

- Definition and importance of sorting data in database management.
- Overview of scenarios where sorting data is essential for effective data analysis and presentation.

## 1.2 Role of the ORDER BY Clause:

- Explanation of the ORDER BY clause and its significance in SQL queries.
- Understanding how the ORDER BY clause facilitates sorting query results based on specified columns.

## 1.3 Syntax of the ORDER BY Clause:

- Exploring the syntax components of the ORDER BY clause, including column names and sorting directions (ASC, DESC).
- Overview of the ORDER BY clause's position within the SELECT statement.

# Chapter 2: Sorting Data by Single Column

## 2.1 Sorting Ascending and Descending:

- Understanding the default sorting behavior of the ORDER BY clause.
- Syntax for specifying ascending (ASC) and descending (DESC) sorting orders.

## 2.2 Sorting Textual Data:

- Techniques for sorting textual data alphabetically using the ORDER BY clause.
- Handling case sensitivity and special characters in text sorting.

## 2.3 Sorting Numeric Data:

- Sorting numeric data in ascending and descending order using the ORDER BY clause.
- Considerations for sorting numeric data with decimal points or negative values.

# Chapter 3: Sorting Data by Multiple Columns

## 3.1 Introduction to Multi-Column Sorting:

- Explanation of multi-column sorting and its role in refining query results.
- Understanding the precedence of column sorting in multi-column ORDER BY clauses.

## 3.2 Sorting Data by Multiple Columns:

- Syntax and examples demonstrating how to sort query results by multiple columns.
- Techniques for specifying primary and secondary sorting criteria.

## 3.3 Handling Null Values in Multi-Column Sorting:

- Strategies for handling null values when sorting data by multiple columns.
- Using NULLS FIRST and NULLS LAST options to control the placement of null values in sorted results.

# Chapter 4: Sorting Data by Expressions and Functions

## 4.1 Sorting Data by Expressions:

- Introduction to sorting data based on expressions or computed values.
- Syntax and examples illustrating how to use expressions in the ORDER BY clause for sorting.

## 4.2 Sorting Data by Functions:

- Leveraging SQL functions for sorting data based on calculated values or transformations.
- Examples demonstrating how to use built-in functions such as CONCAT, DATEPART, and CASE in sorting.

## 4.3 Performance Considerations for Sorting by Expressions and Functions:

- Considerations for performance optimization when sorting data by expressions or functions.
- Techniques for minimizing computational overhead and improving query performance.

# Chapter 5: Sorting Grouped Data with GROUP BY and ORDER BY

## 5.1 Introduction to Grouped Data Sorting:

- Explanation of sorting grouped data in SQL queries.
- Overview of the relationship between GROUP BY and ORDER BY clauses in sorted grouping operations.

## 5.2 Sorting Grouped Data by Aggregate Values:

- Techniques for sorting grouped data based on aggregate function results.
- Examples illustrating how to use ORDER BY in conjunction with GROUP BY for sorted grouping operations.

## 5.3 Performance Optimization for Sorted Grouping:

- Strategies for optimizing performance when sorting grouped data with ORDER BY.
- Indexing, query tuning, and other optimization techniques for efficient sorted grouping operations.

# Chapter 6: Sorting Data with Advanced Techniques

## 6.1 Sorting Hierarchical Data:

- Strategies for sorting hierarchical data structures such as parent-child relationships.
- Recursive queries and common table expressions (CTEs) for sorting hierarchical data in MS SQL Server.

## 6.2 Sorting Pagination Results:

- Techniques for implementing pagination with sorted query results.
- Using OFFSET and FETCH clauses for pagination in sorted queries.

## 6.3 Sorting Data in Specialized Scenarios:

- Handling sorting challenges in specialized scenarios such as time series data, geographical data, and categorical data.
- Best practices and techniques for sorting data in diverse and complex datasets.

# Chapter 7: Best Practices and Performance Optimization

## 7.1 Best Practices for Data Sorting:

- Guidelines for writing efficient and maintainable ORDER BY clauses.
- Considerations for data consistency, readability, and usability in sorted query results.

## 7.2 Performance Optimization Techniques:

- Strategies for optimizing performance when sorting large datasets.
- Indexing, query optimization, and caching techniques for improving sorting performance.

## 7.3 Monitoring and Troubleshooting Sorted Queries:

- Tools and utilities for monitoring sorting operations and diagnosing performance issues.
- Techniques for troubleshooting common sorting-related errors and bottlenecks.

# Mastering Data Sorting in MS SQL Server

In summary, knowing how to use the ORDER BY statement to sort data is crucial for effective data management and query optimization in MS SQL Server. By understanding the differences between sorting syntax, functionality, and best practices, beginners can effectively plan questions and gain insights from their data. With the knowledge and ideas gained in this comprehensive guide, beginners can analyze data in MS SQL Server with confidence, opening up new possibilities in data analysis, review and decision-making.

# Mastering Table Joins: INNER JOIN, LEFT JOIN, and RIGHT JOIN in MS SQL Server

In the world of data management, the ability to retrieve data from multiple tables is crucial for effective data analysis and retrieval. Microsoft SQL Server (MS SQL) provides powerful join tools such as INNER JOIN, LEFT JOIN, and RIGHT JOIN. Each association type has a specific purpose and provides specific functionality for data integration. For someone working with MS SQL libraries, it is important to understand how to use such connections. In this guide, we'll dive into the intricacies of joins, exploring their syntax, functionality, and best practices. Beginners can improve their MS SQL skills by delving into INNER, LEFT and RIGHT JOIN, opening up new possibilities for data management and analysis.

# Chapter 1: Introduction to Table Joins

In this chapter, we'll provide an overview of table joins and their significance in database management. We'll discuss the concept of relational databases, explain why table joins are necessary, and introduce the different types of joins available in MS SQL Server.

## 1.1 Understanding Relational Databases:

- Definition of relational databases and their structure.
- Explanation of tables, rows, columns, and relationships between tables.

## 1.2 Why Table Joins are Necessary:

- Discussing scenarios where data is distributed across multiple tables.
- Exploring the need to combine related data from different tables for analysis.

## 1.3 Overview of Table Join Types:

- Introduction to INNER JOIN, LEFT JOIN, and RIGHT JOIN.
- Differentiating between these join types based on their functionalities and outcomes.

# Chapter 2: INNER JOIN: Combining Matching Rows

In this chapter, we'll focus on INNER JOIN, a fundamental type of table join used to retrieve rows from two tables where there is a match between the specified columns.

## 2.1 Syntax of INNER JOIN:

- Explaining the syntax of INNER JOIN and its components.
- Discussing how to specify the joining condition using the ON clause.

## 2.2 Performing INNER JOIN:

- Providing examples of INNER JOIN to illustrate how it works.
- Demonstrating how to retrieve data from related tables using INNER JOIN.

## 2.3 Use Cases and Best Practices:

- Discussing common scenarios where INNER JOIN is used.
- Providing best practices for optimizing performance and readability when using INNER JOIN.

# Chapter 3: LEFT JOIN: Including All Rows from Left Table

In this chapter, we'll explore LEFT JOIN, a type of table join that returns all rows from the left table and the matching rows from the right table, or NULL values if there is no match.

## 3.1 Syntax of LEFT JOIN:

- Explaining the syntax of LEFT JOIN and its usage.
- Discussing how to handle NULL values in LEFT JOIN results.

## 3.2 Performing LEFT JOIN:

- Providing examples of LEFT JOIN to demonstrate its functionality.
- Illustrating how LEFT JOIN can be used to retrieve data from related tables.

## 3.3 Use Cases and Considerations:

- Discussing scenarios where LEFT JOIN is beneficial, such as retrieving all customers and their orders.
- Highlighting considerations for using LEFT JOIN effectively and avoiding common pitfalls.


# Chapter 4: RIGHT JOIN: Including All Rows from Right Table

In this chapter, we'll delve into RIGHT JOIN, a type of table join that returns all rows from the right table and the matching rows from the left table, or NULL values if there is no match.

## 4.1 Syntax of RIGHT JOIN:

- Explaining the syntax of RIGHT JOIN and its structure.
- Discussing how to specify the joining condition and handle NULL values.

## 4.2 Performing RIGHT JOIN:

- Providing examples of RIGHT JOIN to illustrate its functionality.
- Demonstrating how RIGHT JOIN can be used to retrieve data from related tables.

## 4.3 Use Cases and Comparison with LEFT JOIN:

- Discussing scenarios where RIGHT JOIN is preferred over LEFT JOIN.
- Comparing the outcomes of RIGHT JOIN and LEFT JOIN in different scenarios.

# Chapter 5: FULL JOIN: Including All Rows from Both Tables

In this chapter, we'll explore FULL JOIN, a type of table join that returns all rows from both tables, matching rows from both tables where applicable, and NULL values where there is no match.

## 5.1 Syntax of FULL JOIN:

- Explaining the syntax of FULL JOIN and its components.
- Discussing how to handle NULL values in FULL JOIN results.

## 5.2 Performing FULL JOIN:

- Providing examples of FULL JOIN to demonstrate its functionality.
- Illustrating how FULL JOIN can be used to retrieve data from related tables.

## 5.3 Use Cases and Considerations:

- Discussing scenarios where FULL JOIN is beneficial, such as merging two datasets with overlapping and non-overlapping records.
- Highlighting considerations for using FULL JOIN effectively and avoiding common pitfalls.


# Chapter 6: CROSS JOIN: Generating Cartesian Products

In this chapter, we'll delve into CROSS JOIN, a type of table join that generates the Cartesian product of two tables, combining every row from the first table with every row from the second table.

## 6.1 Syntax of CROSS JOIN:

- Explaining the syntax of CROSS JOIN and its structure.
- Discussing the potential pitfalls of using CROSS JOIN and how to avoid them.

## 6.2 Performing CROSS JOIN:

- Providing examples of CROSS JOIN to illustrate its functionality.
- Demonstrating how CROSS JOIN can be used to generate combinations of data from multiple tables.

## 6.3 Use Cases and Considerations:

- Discussing scenarios where CROSS JOIN is appropriate, such as generating all possible combinations of products and customers.
- Highlighting considerations for using CROSS JOIN effectively and avoiding performance issues.

# Chapter 7: Complex Joining Scenarios: Using Multiple Join Types

In this chapter, we'll explore complex joining scenarios where multiple join types are combined to retrieve data from multiple tables.

## 7.1 Using Multiple JOIN Clauses:

- Explaining how to combine multiple JOIN clauses in a single query.
- Discussing the order of evaluation and the impact on query results.

## 7.2 Nested Joins and Subqueries:

- Introducing nested joins and subqueries for complex data retrieval tasks.
- Providing examples of nested joins and subqueries to illustrate their usage.

## 7.3 Self Joins and Recursive Joins:

- Exploring self-joins and recursive joins for querying hierarchical data structures.
- Demonstrating how to use self-joins and recursive joins in practical scenarios.


# Chapter 8: Joining Tables in Practice: Real-world Examples

In this chapter, we'll apply the concepts learned in previous chapters to real-world examples, demonstrating how to use INNER JOIN, LEFT JOIN, RIGHT JOIN, FULL JOIN, and CROSS JOIN in practical scenarios.

## 8.1 Joining Tables for Data Analysis:

- Demonstrating how to join tables to perform data analysis tasks, such as generating reports and summarizing information.

## 8.2 Joining Tables for Data Migration:

- Exploring how to use table joins during data migration and data integration projects.
- Discussing strategies for mapping and transforming data between different tables.

## 8.3 Joining Tables for Application Development:

- Illustrating how to use table joins in application development scenarios, such as building web applications or business intelligence solutions.

# Mastering Grouping Data with GROUP BY in MS SQL Server

In MS SQL Server, the GROUP BY clause is a powerful tool used to aggregate data and organize it into logical groups based on one or more columns. Mastering the GROUP BY clause allows you to efficiently analyze data and derive insights from large datasets. Here's a comprehensive guide to mastering GROUP BY in MS SQL Server.

1. **Syntax**: The basic syntax of the GROUP BY clause is straightforward. After the SELECT statement, specify the columns you want to group by, followed by the GROUP BY keyword. For example:

```
SELECT column1, column2, aggregate_function(column3) FROM table_name

GROUP BY column1, column2;
```

2. **Aggregation Functions**: When using GROUP BY, you typically use aggregate functions like COUNT, SUM, AVG, MIN, and MAX to perform calculations on groups of data. These functions operate on the rows within each group to produce a single result per group.

3. **Filtering Groups**: You can apply the HAVING clause after the GROUP BY clause to filter groups based on aggregate conditions. This allows you to exclude certain groups from the result set based on aggregate values.

4. **Ordering Groups**: You can specify the ORDER BY clause to sort the groups based on certain criteria. This is especially useful when you want to see the groups in a specific order, such as sorting them by the result of an aggregate function.

5. **Grouping Sets and Rollup**: MS SQL Server supports advanced grouping techniques like GROUPING SETS and ROLLUP, which allow you to specify multiple grouping sets within a single query. This is particularly handy when you want to aggregate data at different levels of granularity simultaneously.

6. **NULL Handling**: When grouping data, NULL values in the grouped columns are treated as a single group. If you want to treat NULL values differently, you can use the GROUPING SETS or ROLLUP feature along with the GROUPING function to distinguish between NULL and non-NULL groups.

7. **Performance Considerations**: Efficiently using GROUP BY is crucial for performance, especially when dealing with large datasets. Ensure that you have proper indexing on the columns involved in grouping and aggregations to optimize query performance.

8. **Joins with Grouping**: GROUP BY can be used in conjunction with joins to aggregate data from multiple tables. When joining tables, ensure that you properly specify the join conditions and group by the appropriate columns to avoid incorrect results.

Mastering the GROUP BY clause in MS SQL Server enables you to perform complex data analysis tasks efficiently. By understanding its syntax, various aggregation functions, advanced grouping techniques, and performance considerations, you can manipulate and extract valuable insights from your datasets effectively.

# Chapter 1: Understanding the Basics of GROUP BY

## 1.1 Introduction to GROUP BY:

- Definition and purpose of the GROUP BY clause in SQL.
- Overview of how GROUP BY facilitates data grouping and aggregation.

## 1.2 Syntax of GROUP BY:

- Explaining the syntax of the GROUP BY clause and its components.
- Discussing how to use GROUP BY in conjunction with other SQL clauses.

## 1.3 Aggregating Data with Aggregate Functions:

- Introduction to aggregate functions such as SUM, AVG, COUNT, MIN, and MAX.
- Discussing how aggregate functions are used in conjunction with GROUP BY.

# Chapter 2: Grouping Data with Simple GROUP BY Queries

## 2.1 Basic Usage of GROUP BY:

- Providing examples of simple GROUP BY queries to group data by a single column.
- Demonstrating how to use aggregate functions to calculate summary statistics within each group.

## 2.2 Filtering Grouped Data with the HAVING Clause:

- Explaining the purpose of the HAVING clause in filtering grouped data.
- Discussing how to use the HAVING clause to specify conditions for grouped data.

## 2.3 Sorting Grouped Data with ORDER BY:

- Exploring how to sort grouped data using the ORDER BY clause.
- Discussing the impact of sorting on the presentation of grouped data.

# Chapter 3: Advanced Grouping Techniques

## 3.1 Grouping Data by Multiple Columns:

- Discussing how to group data by multiple columns using GROUP BY.
- Providing examples of complex GROUP BY queries with multiple grouping criteria.

## 3.2 Using Grouping Sets:

- Introduction to grouping sets for generating multiple levels of grouping within a single query.
- Explaining the syntax and usage of grouping sets in MS SQL Server.

## 3.3 Rollup and Cube Operations:

- Exploring rollup and cube operations for generating subtotal and grand total rows in grouped data.
- Discussing how to use rollup and cube with GROUP BY to create hierarchical summaries.

# Chapter 4: Grouping Data Across Time Intervals

## 4.1 Grouping Data by Date Parts:

- Discussing techniques for grouping data by date parts such as year, month, day, etc.
- Providing examples of date-based grouping using the DATEPART function.

## 4.2 Using Date Functions for Time Intervals:

- Exploring date functions such as DATEADD and DATEDIFF for defining custom time intervals.
- Demonstrating how to group data into time intervals using date functions.

## 4.3 Aggregating Time-Series Data:

- Discussing strategies for aggregating time-series data using GROUP BY and date functions.
- Providing examples of common use cases for aggregating time-series data.

# Chapter 5: Grouping Data with Joins and Subqueries

## 5.1 Grouping Joined Data:

- Exploring how to group data from multiple tables using JOIN operations.
- Discussing considerations and best practices for grouping joined data.

## 5.2 Grouping Data with Subqueries:

- Introduction to subqueries for grouping data within a subquery before joining with other tables.
- Providing examples of using subqueries for grouped data retrieval.

## 5.3 Optimizing Grouped Queries:

- Discussing strategies for optimizing queries involving grouped data.
- Exploring indexing, query tuning, and other optimization techniques.

# Chapter 6: Practical Applications of Grouping Data

## 6.1 Analyzing Sales Data:

- Demonstrating how to group sales data by product, region, or time period for analysis.
- Discussing techniques for calculating sales totals, averages, and other metrics.

## 6.2 Summarizing Employee Data:

- Exploring how to group employee data by department, job title, or hire date for reporting purposes.
- Discussing techniques for calculating employee counts, salaries, and other statistics.

## 6.3 Visualizing Grouped Data:

- Discussing tools and techniques for visualizing grouped data, such as charts and graphs.
- Exploring integration with data visualization tools for enhanced data analysis.

# Chapter 7: Best Practices and Performance Optimization

## 7.1 Best Practices for Grouping Data:

- Providing guidelines for writing efficient and readable GROUP BY queries.
- Discussing considerations for data integrity, query design, and optimization.

## 7.2 Performance Optimization Techniques:

- Exploring strategies for optimizing performance when grouping large datasets. Discussing indexing, query tuning, and other optimization techniques.

## 7.3 Error Handling and Troubleshooting:

- Providing tips for troubleshooting common issues and errors related to grouping data. Discussing strategies for handling NULL values, ambiguous column names, and other grouping-related problems.

# Mastering the Art of Grouping Data with GROUP BY

In conclusion, mastering the GROUP BY clause is very important for anyone working with MS SQL databases. By understanding its syntax, functionality, and best practices, beginners can group and aggregate data to gain insight and make informed decisions. With the knowledge and ideas gained from this comprehensive guide, beginners can confidently manage and analyze data in MS SQL Server, unlocking new possibilities for making data decisions and achieving business goals.

# Mastering Subqueries: An Introduction to Subqueries in MS SQL Server

The ability to extract, manage and analyze data is important in data management. Microsoft SQL Server (MS SQL) provides many tools and functions to perform these tasks, and one powerful tool is subqueries. Subqueries, also known as nested queries or inner queries, allow SQL developers to query within a query, allowing complex information to be retrieved and processed. In this guide, we will examine the basics of subqueries in MS SQL Server, examining their syntax, types, and practical applications. Whether you're new to SQL or an expert looking to improve your skills, this guide will provide you with the knowledge and techniques you need to implement these queries in MS SQL Server.

Subqueries in MS SQL Server are powerful tools for querying data from one or more tables dynamically within another query. They are enclosed within parentheses and can be used in various parts of a SQL statement, such as the SELECT, FROM, WHERE, or HAVING clauses.

A subquery can return a single value, a single row, multiple rows, or even an entire result set, depending on its purpose within the main query. They are particularly useful for complex filtering, joining, or aggregating data.

Common types of subqueries include:

1. Scalar subqueries: Return a single value and can be used in expressions.
2. Single-row subqueries: Return one row of data and are often used in comparison operations.
3. Multi-row subqueries: Return multiple rows of data and can be used with operators like IN, ANY, or ALL.
4. Correlated subqueries: Reference columns from the outer query, making them dependent on the outer query's execution.

Mastering subqueries in MS SQL Server opens up possibilities for writing more efficient and flexible SQL queries to retrieve, manipulate, and analyze data.

# Chapter 1: Understanding Subqueries

## 1.1 Introduction to Subqueries:

  - Definition and purpose of subqueries in SQL.
  - Overview of how subqueries are used to perform nested queries within SQL statements.

## 1.2 Types of Subqueries:

  - Exploring the different types of subqueries, including scalar subqueries, single-row subqueries, and multi-row subqueries.
  - Discussing the characteristics and use cases for each type of subquery.

## 1.3 Subquery Syntax:

  - Understanding the syntax of subqueries, including the placement of subqueries within SQL statements and the use of subquery operators.


# Chapter 2: Scalar Subqueries: Retrieving Single Values

## 2.1 Introduction to Scalar Subqueries:

  - Definition and characteristics of scalar subqueries.
  - Exploring how scalar subqueries are used to retrieve a single value from the database.

## 2.2 Scalar Subquery Examples:

  - Providing examples of scalar subqueries to demonstrate their usage in practical scenarios.
  - Discussing how scalar subqueries can be used in SELECT, WHERE, and other clauses.

## 2.3 Best Practices for Using Scalar Subqueries:

  - Guidelines for writing efficient and readable scalar subqueries.
  - Discussing considerations for optimizing performance and avoiding common pitfalls.

# Chapter 3: Single-Row Subqueries: Retrieving Single Rows

## 3.1 Introduction to Single-Row Subqueries:

- Definition and characteristics of single-row subqueries.
- Exploring how single-row subqueries are used to retrieve a single row from the database.

## 3.2 Single-Row Subquery Examples:

- Providing examples of single-row subqueries to demonstrate their usage in practical scenarios.
- Discussing how single-row subqueries can be used in SELECT, WHERE, and other clauses.

## 3.3 Best Practices for Using Single-Row Subqueries:

- Guidelines for writing efficient and readable single-row subqueries.
- Discussing considerations for optimizing performance and avoiding common pitfalls.

# Chapter 4: Multi-Row Subqueries: Retrieving Multiple Rows

## 4.1 Introduction to Multi-Row Subqueries:

- Definition and characteristics of multi-row subqueries.
- Exploring how multi-row subqueries are used to retrieve multiple rows from the database.

## 4.2 Multi-Row Subquery Examples:

- Providing examples of multi-row subqueries to demonstrate their usage in practical scenarios.
- Discussing how multi-row subqueries can be used in SELECT, WHERE, and other clauses.

## 4.3 Best Practices for Using Multi-Row Subqueries:

- Guidelines for writing efficient and readable multi-row subqueries.
- Discussing considerations for optimizing performance and avoiding common pitfalls.

# Chapter 5: Correlated Subqueries: Dependent Subqueries

## 5.1 Introduction to Correlated Subqueries:

- Definition and characteristics of correlated subqueries.
- Exploring how correlated subqueries are used to reference outer query columns within inner queries.

## 5.2 Correlated Subquery Examples:

- Providing examples of correlated subqueries to demonstrate their usage in practical scenarios.
- Discussing how correlated subqueries can be used to filter results based on outer query values.

## 5.3 Best Practices for Using Correlated Subqueries:

- Guidelines for writing efficient and readable correlated subqueries.
- Discussing considerations for optimizing performance and avoiding common pitfalls.

# Chapter 6: Subqueries in Different Clauses

## 6.1 Subqueries in SELECT Clause:

- Exploring how subqueries can be used in the SELECT clause to retrieve computed values or aggregate data.

## 6.2 Subqueries in WHERE Clause:

- Discussing how subqueries can be used in the WHERE clause to filter results based on the outcome of inner queries.

## 6.3 Subqueries in FROM Clause:

- Exploring how subqueries can be used in the FROM clause to create virtual tables for further processing.

# Chapter 7: Practical Applications of Subqueries

## 7.1 Using Subqueries for Data Retrieval:

- Demonstrating how subqueries can be used to retrieve specific subsets of data from the database.

## 7.2 Using Subqueries for Data Modification:

- Exploring how subqueries can be used to modify data in the database, including INSERT, UPDATE, and DELETE operations.

## 7.3 Using Subqueries for Data Analysis:

- Discussing how subqueries can be used for data analysis tasks, such as calculating aggregates or identifying patterns in the data.

# Chapter 8: Advanced Subquery Techniques

## 8.1 Nested Subqueries:

- Exploring nested subqueries, where subqueries are nested within other subqueries, for advanced data manipulation tasks.

## 8.2 Using Common Table Expressions (CTEs) with Subqueries:

- Discussing how common table expressions (CTEs) can be used in conjunction with subqueries for improved readability and performance.

## 8.3 Subqueries with EXISTS and NOT EXISTS Operators:

- Exploring how EXISTS and NOT EXISTS operators can be used with subqueries to check for the existence of rows in a correlated subquery.

# Chapter 9: Best Practices and Performance Optimization

## 9.1 Best Practices for Writing Subqueries:

- Providing guidelines for writing efficient and maintainable subqueries.
- Discussing considerations for readability, performance, and optimization.

## 9.2 Performance Optimization Techniques:

- Exploring strategies for optimizing the performance of subqueries, including indexing, query tuning, and rewriting queries.

## 9.3 Error Handling and Troubleshooting:

- Providing tips for troubleshooting common issues and errors related to subqueries.
- Discussing strategies for handling NULL values, ambiguous column names, and other subquery-related problems.

# Mastering Subqueries in MS SQL Server

As a result, mastering subqueries is crucial for anyone working with MS SQL databases. By understanding the different types of subqueries, their syntax, and data usage, beginners can effectively use subqueries to manage and analyze data. With the knowledge and ideas gained from this comprehensive guide, beginners can confidently use questions to solve complex data-related problems, opening up new possibilities for database management and analysis in MS SQL Server.

# Demystifying Indexes: Types and Usage in MS SQL Server

In the field of data management, optimizing query performance is important to ensure good retrieval and use of data. Indexes play an important role in speeding up database operations by providing quick access to data stored in tables. Understanding the types of metrics available in Microsoft SQL Server (MS SQL) and their usage is important for administrators and developers. In this guide, we will delve into the intricacies of indexes in MS SQL Server, exploring their types and best practices for creating and using them. Beginners can increase the efficiency of SQL queries and improve their MS SQL skills by mastering indexes.

# Chapter 1: Introduction to Indexes

1.1 Understanding Indexes:

 - Definition of indexes and their significance in database management.
 - Overview of how indexes improve query performance by facilitating rapid data retrieval.

1.2 Types of Indexes in MS SQL Server:

 - Introduction to different types of indexes, including clustered, non-clustered, and unique indexes.
 - Explaining the differences between primary and secondary indexes.

1.3 Importance of Index Selection:

 - Discussing factors to consider when selecting indexes, such as query patterns, data distribution, and storage constraints.

# Chapter 2: Clustered Indexes: Organizing Data for Efficiency

## 2.1 Overview of Clustered Indexes:

- Explanation of clustered indexes and their role in organizing data within a table.
- Discussing how clustered indexes determine the physical order of rows in a table.

## 2.2 Creating Clustered Indexes:

- Step-by-step guide to creating clustered indexes using SQL Server Management Studio (SSMS) or Transact-SQL (T-SQL).
- Best practices for choosing the appropriate columns for clustered indexes.

## 2.3 Benefits and Limitations:

- Exploring the benefits of clustered indexes, such as improved data retrieval speed and efficient range scans.
- Discussing limitations and considerations for using clustered indexes, such as impact on data modification operations.

# Chapter 3: Non-Clustered Indexes: Optimizing Query Performance

## 3.1 Understanding Non-Clustered Indexes:

- Definition of non-clustered indexes and their role in enhancing query performance.
- Explaining how non-clustered indexes store a separate copy of indexed columns and pointers to the corresponding rows.

## 3.2 Creating Non-Clustered Indexes:

- Step-by-step guide to creating non-clustered indexes using SSMS or T-SQL.
- Discussing considerations for selecting the appropriate columns for non-clustered indexes.

## 3.3 Use Cases and Best Practices:

- Providing examples of scenarios where non-clustered indexes are beneficial, such as filtering and sorting operations.
- Best practices for optimizing query performance with non-clustered indexes, including index maintenance and monitoring.

# Chapter 4: Unique Indexes: Enforcing Data Integrity

## 4.1 Introduction to Unique Indexes:

- Explanation of unique indexes and their role in enforcing data integrity constraints.
- Discussing how unique indexes prevent duplicate values in indexed columns.

## 4.2 Creating Unique Indexes:

- Step-by-step guide to creating unique indexes using SSMS or T-SQL.
- Exploring options for defining unique constraints and handling NULL values in unique indexes.

## 4.3 Practical Applications:

- Discussing practical applications of unique indexes, such as enforcing primary key constraints and ensuring data uniqueness in critical columns.


# Chapter 5: Composite Indexes: Optimizing Complex Queries

## 5.1 Understanding Composite Indexes:

- Definition of composite indexes and their ability to index multiple columns in a table.
- Explaining how composite indexes can improve query performance for complex filtering and sorting operations.

## 5.2 Creating Composite Indexes:

- Step-by-step guide to creating composite indexes with multiple columns using SSMS or T-SQL.
- Discussing considerations for column order and index key selection in composite indexes.

## 5.3 Performance Considerations:

- Exploring performance considerations and trade-offs associated with composite indexes, such as index size and maintenance overhead.

# Chapter 6: Covering Indexes: Improving Query Efficiency

## 6.1 Introduction to Covering Indexes:

- Definition of covering indexes and their role in improving query efficiency by including all columns required for a query.

## 6.2 Creating Covering Indexes:

- Step-by-step guide to creating covering indexes to optimize specific query patterns.
- Explaining how to determine which columns to include in covering indexes based on query requirements.

## 6.3 Best Practices and Considerations:

- Providing best practices for using covering indexes effectively, such as minimizing index size and avoiding over-indexing.
- Discussing considerations for index maintenance and monitoring in covering indexes.

# Chapter 7: Monitoring and Maintaining Indexes

## 7.1 Index Maintenance Strategies:

- Exploring strategies for index maintenance, including index rebuilds, reorganization, and statistics updates.
- Discussing the importance of index fragmentation analysis and its impact on query performance.

## 7.2 Monitoring Index Performance:

- Introducing tools and techniques for monitoring index performance, such as SQL Server Profiler and Dynamic Management Views (DMVs).
- Explaining how to identify and troubleshoot common index-related performance issues.

## 7.3 Index Design Best Practices:

- Summarizing best practices for index design, including index creation, modification, and removal.
- Discussing the importance of ongoing optimization and refinement of index strategies based on changing workload patterns.

# Mastering Indexes for Enhanced Query Performance

In summary, mastering indexes is important for optimizing query performance and maximizing the efficiency of your MS SQL Server database. Beginners can increase the speed and performance of SQL queries by understanding the types of indexes available and their proper use. Beginners can safely create, implement and manage performance metrics in the MS SQL Server environment with the knowledge and techniques gained from this guide

# Mastering Indexes in MS SQL Server: Types, Usage, and Best Practices

In Microsoft SQL Server, indexes play a critical role in enhancing query performance by facilitating efficient data retrieval. There are several types of indexes, including clustered, non-clustered, unique, and filtered indexes.

Clustered indexes dictate the physical order of data in a table, while non-clustered indexes store a separate structure pointing to the data rows. Unique indexes ensure data integrity by enforcing uniqueness constraints, while filtered indexes optimize query performance by indexing a subset of data based on specified filter conditions.

To maximize the effectiveness of indexes, it's essential to follow best practices. This includes identifying and creating indexes based on query patterns and workload analysis, avoiding over-indexing to prevent unnecessary overhead, regularly monitoring and maintaining indexes to ensure optimal performance, and considering the impact of index maintenance tasks on system resources.

Additionally, utilizing index management features such as the Database Engine Tuning Advisor (DTA) or Execution Plan analysis can help identify opportunities for index optimization. It's also crucial to keep index statistics up-to-date to ensure the query optimizer makes informed decisions.

By understanding the various types of indexes available, implementing best practices for index creation and maintenance, and leveraging appropriate tools for optimization, SQL Server users can significantly improve query performance and overall system efficiency.

# Chapter 1: Introduction to Indexes

## 1.1 What are Indexes?

- Definition of indexes in the context of database management.
- Explanation of how indexes improve query performance by facilitating faster data retrieval.

## 1.2 Importance of Indexes:

- Discussing the significance of indexes in optimizing query execution time and reducing resource consumption.
- Exploring the impact of indexes on overall system efficiency and user experience.

## 1.3 Basic Indexing Concepts:

- Introducing fundamental indexing concepts such as key columns, leaf nodes, and index structures.
- Explaining how indexes are organized and stored in MS SQL Server.

# Chapter 2: Types of Indexes in MS SQL Server

## 2.1 Clustered Indexes:

- Defining clustered indexes and their role in defining the physical order of data within a table.
- Exploring scenarios where clustered indexes are beneficial and their implications on data retrieval.

## 2.2 Non-Clustered Indexes:

- Explaining non-clustered indexes and their ability to provide an alternative path for data retrieval.
- Discussing the advantages and limitations of non-clustered indexes compared to clustered indexes.

## 2.3 Unique Indexes:

- Introducing unique indexes and their role in enforcing data integrity constraints.
- Exploring scenarios where unique indexes are useful and their impact on query performance.

## 2.4 Filtered Indexes:

- Defining filtered indexes and their ability to index a subset of data based on specified filter conditions.

- Discussing the advantages of filtered indexes in optimizing query performance for specific data subsets.

# Chapter 3: Creating and Managing Indexes

## 3.1 Index Creation Syntax:

- Providing an overview of the syntax for creating indexes in MS SQL Server.
- Explaining the options and parameters available for customizing index creation.

## 3.2 Index Maintenance:

- Discussing the importance of index maintenance for ensuring optimal performance.
- Exploring techniques for monitoring index health and detecting fragmentation.

## 3.3 Index Rebuilding and Reorganizing:

- Explaining the concepts of index rebuilding and reorganizing for managing index fragmentation.
- Discussing best practices for scheduling and performing index maintenance tasks.

# Chapter 4: Indexing Strategies and Best Practices

## 4.1 Identifying Indexing Opportunities:

- Discussing strategies for identifying potential candidates for indexing based on query patterns and access patterns.
- Exploring techniques for analyzing query execution plans to identify missing or underutilized indexes.

## 4.2 Index Design Considerations:

- Discussing factors to consider when designing indexes, such as selectivity, cardinality, and data distribution.
- Exploring techniques for designing composite indexes to optimize query performance for multiple columns.

## 4.3 Avoiding Over-Indexing:

- Explaining the drawbacks of over-indexing and its impact on data modification operations and storage overhead.
- Discussing strategies for balancing the need for indexes with the associated costs and trade-offs.

# Chapter 5: Advanced Indexing Techniques

## 5.1 Covering Indexes:

- Introducing covering indexes and their ability to satisfy query requirements without accessing the underlying table.
- Exploring scenarios where covering indexes are beneficial and their implications on query performance.

## 5.2 Indexing Computed Columns:

- Discussing techniques for indexing computed columns to improve query performance for calculated expressions.
- Exploring considerations and limitations when indexing computed columns.

## 5.3 Indexing Temporal Data:

- Exploring techniques for indexing temporal data, such as date and time columns.
- Discussing strategies for optimizing queries involving date range predicates and date calculations.

# Chapter 6: Monitoring and Troubleshooting Indexes

## 6.1 Index Performance Monitoring:

- Discussing techniques for monitoring index usage, fragmentation levels, and query performance.
- Exploring built-in tools and dynamic management views for tracking index health and performance.

## 6.2 Index Fragmentation Analysis:

- Explaining how to detect and analyze index fragmentation using dynamic management views and performance monitoring utilities.
- Discussing strategies for addressing index fragmentation and optimizing query performance.

## 6.3 Troubleshooting Common Indexing Issues:

- Discussing common issues and challenges related to index usage and performance.
- Providing troubleshooting tips and techniques for resolving indexing-related problems.

# Chapter 7: Real-world Applications and Case Studies

## 7.1 Indexing Best Practices in Action:

- Presenting real-world scenarios where indexing best practices have been applied to improve query performance.
- Discussing the challenges faced, strategies implemented, and outcomes achieved through effective indexing.

## 7.2 Case Studies:

- Presenting case studies of organizations that have successfully implemented indexing strategies to optimize query performance.
- Exploring the before-and-after performance metrics and the impact of indexing on overall system efficiency.

# Mastering Indexes for Enhanced Query Performance

In summary, mastering indexes is important for optimizing MS SQL Server query performance and improving overall system efficiency. Beginners can improve their SQL skills and achieve success in database management by understanding the types and uses of indexes, using indexing strategies and best practices, and managing health and performance. Thanks to the knowledge and techniques gained in this comprehensive guide, beginners can confidently use metrics to improve question performance and contribute to success in the use of data, information and technology.

# Mastering Efficient Query Writing in MS SQL Server

In the world of data management, well-written queries are crucial for maximizing efficiency and optimizing resource usage. Microsoft SQL Server (MS SQL) provides a powerful SQL language that allows users to retrieve, manage and analyze data efficiently. But knowing how to write effective queries requires a deep understanding of SQL syntax, query optimization techniques, and best practices. In this guide, we will help beginners improve their SQL skills and achieve great results in database management by examining techniques for writing effective queries in MS SQL Server.

# Chapter 1: Understanding Query Efficiency

## 1.1 Importance of Query Efficiency:

- Discussing the significance of writing efficient queries for improving application performance and user experience.
- Exploring the impact of inefficient queries on database server resources and overall system scalability.

## 1.2 Factors Affecting Query Performance:

- Identifying key factors that influence query performance, including indexing, query structure, data volume, and server configuration.
- Discussing how each factor contributes to overall query execution time and resource utilization.

## 1.3 Benefits of Writing Efficient Queries:

- Discussing the benefits of writing efficient queries, such as faster response times, reduced server load, and improved application scalability.
- Exploring real-world examples of organizations that have achieved significant performance improvements through query optimization efforts.

# Chapter 2: Writing Structured and Readable Queries

## 2.1 SQL Query Structure:

- Explaining the basic structure of SQL queries, including SELECT, FROM, WHERE, GROUP BY, HAVING, and ORDER BY clauses.
- Discussing best practices for organizing and formatting SQL queries for readability and maintainability.

## 2.2 Selecting Necessary Columns:

- Discussing the importance of selecting only the necessary columns in SELECT queries to minimize data retrieval overhead.
- Exploring techniques for avoiding unnecessary columns and calculations in query results.

## 2.3 Avoiding Nested Queries:

- Explaining the drawbacks of nested queries and their impact on query performance.
- Discussing alternatives to nested queries, such as joins and subqueries, to improve query efficiency.

# Chapter 3: Utilizing Indexes for Query Optimization

## 3.1 Understanding Indexing:

- Providing an overview of indexing and its role in query optimization.
- Explaining the types of indexes available in MS SQL Server, including clustered and non-clustered indexes.

## 3.2 Choosing the Right Indexes:

- Discussing factors to consider when selecting indexes for tables, such as query patterns, data distribution, and table size.
- Exploring techniques for identifying optimal indexing strategies to improve query performance.

## 3.3 Indexing Best Practices:

- Providing guidelines for creating and maintaining indexes to ensure optimal query performance.
- Discussing techniques for monitoring index usage, identifying unused indexes, and optimizing index fragmentation.

# Chapter 4: Optimizing Query Execution

## 4.1 Query Rewriting and Optimization:

- Exploring techniques for rewriting queries to improve performance, such as restructuring joins and predicates.
- Discussing how to optimize queries for specific use cases and workload patterns.

## 4.2 Using Query Execution Plans:

- Explaining how to utilize query execution plans to analyze query performance and identify areas for optimization.
- Discussing techniques for interpreting query execution plans and optimizing query performance based on their insights.

## 4.3 Parallel Query Execution:

- Discussing the benefits and drawbacks of parallel query execution in MS SQL Server.
- Exploring techniques for enabling and controlling parallelism to improve query performance.

# Chapter 5: Leveraging Query Optimization Techniques

## 5.1 Using Query Hints:

- Explaining how query hints can be used to influence query execution behavior and improve performance.
- Discussing common query hints, such as INDEX, FORCESEEK, and LOOP JOIN, and their impact on query performance.

## 5.2 Covering Indexes:

- Introducing covering indexes and their ability to satisfy query requirements without accessing the underlying table.
- Exploring scenarios where covering indexes are beneficial and their implications on query performance.

## 5.3 Caching and Query Performance:

- Discussing techniques for implementing query caching at the application and database levels to improve performance.
- Exploring strategies for leveraging cached query plans and data to minimize resource usage and improve response times.

# Chapter 6: Testing and Benchmarking Queries

## 6.1 Importance of Query Testing:

- Explaining the importance of testing queries under realistic conditions to ensure optimal performance.
- Discussing the benefits of benchmarking queries against predefined performance criteria.

## 6.2 Techniques for Query Testing:

- Providing guidelines for designing and executing query tests in a controlled environment.
- Discussing techniques for measuring query performance and identifying areas for improvement.

## 6.3 Iterative Query Optimization:

- Exploring the iterative process of query optimization and refinement.
- Discussing how to analyze test results, make adjustments to queries, and retest for performance improvements.

# Chapter 7: Real-world Applications and Case Studies

## 7.1 Query Optimization Best Practices in Action:

 - Presenting real-world scenarios where query optimization techniques have been applied to improve performance.
 - Discussing the challenges faced, strategies implemented, and outcomes achieved through effective query optimization.

## 7.2 Case Studies:

 - Presenting case studies of organizations that have successfully optimized their queries to achieve significant performance gains.
 - Exploring the before-and-after performance metrics and the impact of query optimization on overall system efficiency.

# Mastering Efficient Query Writing

In conclusion, knowing how to write effective queries is crucial for beginners to master the full capabilities of MS SQL Server. Beginners can improve their SQL skills and complement what is useful in database management by understanding optimization concepts, using indexing techniques, optimizing query execution, and rigorously testing and benchmarking queries. With the knowledge and ideas gained from this comprehensive guide, beginners can confidently write effective surveys that provide fast and reliable results, ultimately supporting the processing of information using information and systems.

# Harnessing Execution Plans for Query Optimization in MS SQL Server

In the world of database management, optimizing query performance is important to ensure efficient data retrieval and processing. Microsoft SQL Server (MS SQL) provides a powerful tool called execution planning that provides insight into how queries will be executed and helps identify optimization opportunities. However, for those new to query development in MS SQL Server, it is important to understand how to properly define and use execution plans. In this guide, we will examine the intricacies of planning success, exploring their meanings, interpretations and use of optimization questions. By completing the project, beginners can improve their SQL skills and achieve great results in database management.

# Chapter 1: Introduction to Execution Plans

## 1.1 What are Execution Plans?

- Definition of execution plans in the context of MS SQL Server.
- Explanation of how execution plans provide a roadmap for query execution.

## 1.2 Importance of Execution Plans:

- Discussing the significance of execution plans in query optimization and performance tuning.
- Exploring how execution plans help identify inefficient query patterns and optimize query execution.

## 1.3 Generating Execution Plans:

- Explaining the process of generating execution plans in MS SQL Server.
- Discussing different methods for viewing and analyzing execution plans, including graphical and text-based formats.

# Chapter 2: Understanding Execution Plan Components

## 2.1 Query Operators and Data Flow:

- Explaining common query operators used in execution plans, such as scans, seeks, joins, and sorts.
- Discussing how data flows between operators during query execution.

## 2.2 Access Methods:

- Exploring different access methods used to retrieve data from tables and indexes, including table scans, index scans, and index seeks.
- Discussing the factors that influence the choice of access methods in execution plans.

## 2.3 Predicate Evaluation and Filtering:

- Explaining how predicates are evaluated and applied to filter rows during query execution.
- Discussing techniques for optimizing predicate evaluation and reducing the number of rows processed.

# Chapter 3: Interpreting Execution Plans

## 3.1 Reading Execution Plan Icons and Symbols:

- Explaining the meaning of icons and symbols used in execution plans, such as arrows, shapes, and colors.
- Providing a guide to interpreting common symbols and understanding their implications for query performance.

## 3.2 Analyzing Execution Plan Properties:

- Discussing the properties and attributes associated with execution plan operators.
- Exploring how to interpret execution plan properties to identify performance bottlenecks and optimization opportunities.

## 3.3 Identifying Performance Issues:

- Exploring common performance issues and inefficiencies identified through execution plans, such as table scans, nested loops, and excessive sorting.
- Discussing techniques for diagnosing and addressing performance issues based on execution plan analysis.

# Chapter 4: Query Optimization Strategies

## 4.1 Index Utilization:

- Exploring how execution plans indicate index usage and access methods.
- Discussing strategies for optimizing index usage to improve query performance.

## 4.2 Join Optimization:

- Discussing join algorithms and techniques for optimizing join operations in execution plans.
- Exploring strategies for choosing the most efficient join type based on query requirements and data characteristics.

## 4.3 Predicate Pushdown and Filter Order:

- Explaining the concept of predicate pushdown and its impact on query performance.
- Discussing techniques for optimizing filter order and predicate evaluation to minimize row processing.

# Chapter 5: Utilizing Execution Plans for Optimization

## 5.1 Plan Guides and Query Plan Forcing:

- Exploring techniques for guiding query optimization using plan guides and query plan forcing.
- Discussing scenarios where plan guides can be used to override default optimization behavior and improve query performance.

## 5.2 Query Plan Caching and Reuse:

- Discussing the benefits of query plan caching and reuse in improving query performance.
- Exploring techniques for promoting plan reuse and avoiding unnecessary plan compilation.

## 5.3 Plan Stability and Plan Freezing:

- Explaining the concept of plan stability and its importance in maintaining consistent query performance.
- Discussing techniques for freezing execution plans to prevent plan regression and performance degradation.

# Chapter 6: Advanced Execution Plan Analysis

## 6.1 Plan Comparison and Plan Guides:

- Exploring techniques for comparing multiple execution plans and identifying performance differences.
- Discussing how to use plan guides to enforce plan consistency and optimize query performance across different environments.

## 6.2 Extended Events and Query Store:

- Introducing extended events and query store features for capturing and analyzing query execution data.
- Discussing how extended events and query store can be used to monitor execution plan changes and track query performance over time.

## 6.3 Dynamic Management Views (DMVs):

- Exploring dynamic management views (DMVs) for querying execution plan-related metadata and performance metrics.
- Discussing common DMVs used for execution plan analysis and optimization.

# Chapter 7: Real-world Applications and Case Studies

## 7.1 Execution Plan Optimization Best Practices:

- Presenting real-world scenarios where execution plan analysis and optimization techniques have been applied to improve query performance.
- Discussing the challenges faced, strategies implemented, and outcomes achieved through effective execution plan optimization.

## 7.2 Case Studies:

- Presenting case studies of organizations that have successfully optimized their queries using execution plan analysis.
- Exploring the before-and-after performance metrics and the impact of execution plan optimization on overall system efficiency.

# Mastering Execution Plans for Query Optimization

In summary, knowledge of execution plans is necessary for beginners to improve query performance and get good results in MS SQL Server. By understanding the details of the success plan, identifying its components, and using optimization strategies based on the analysis of the success plan, beginners can improve their SQL skills and contribute to the success of data using databases and systems. Beginners can safely use the success plan for optimization questions and achieve the best performance in their management with the knowledge and ideas gained in this comprehensive guide.

# Mastering Database Statistics and Fragmentation Management in MS SQL Server

Effective management in this world of data management requires good data analysis and fragmentation control. Microsoft SQL Server (MS SQL) relies on accurate statistics to create efficient plans, and crashes can reduce performance by causing unnecessary disk I/O and resource usage. For beginners, understanding how to manage database statistics and partitioning is crucial to demonstrate the efficiency and stability of MS SQL Server. In this guide, we will examine techniques for managing data statistics and classification to help beginners improve their SQL skills and optimize data in MS SQL Server.

# Chapter 1: Understanding Database Statistics

## 1.1 Importance of Database Statistics:

- Discussing the significance of database statistics in query optimization and performance tuning.
- Exploring how accurate statistics enable the query optimizer to make informed decisions about query execution.

## 1.2 Types of Database Statistics:

- Introducing different types of statistics in MS SQL Server, including column statistics, index statistics, and system statistics.
- Explaining how each type of statistic contributes to query optimization and performance.

## 1.3 Automatic and Manual Statistics Updates:

- Exploring the mechanisms for updating database statistics automatically and manually in MS SQL Server.
- Discussing the factors that trigger automatic statistics updates and when manual updates may be necessary.

# Chapter 2: Managing Database Statistics

## 2.1 Statistics Maintenance Tasks:

- Discussing best practices for maintaining database statistics to ensure accuracy and relevance.
- Exploring techniques for scheduling automatic statistics updates and monitoring statistics health.

## 2.2 Statistics Sampling:

- Explaining the concept of statistics sampling and its impact on query optimization.
- Discussing different sampling methods available in MS SQL Server and when to use each method.

## 2.3 Statistics Cardinality and Histograms:

- Exploring statistics cardinality and histograms and their role in estimating row counts and data distribution.
- Discussing how to interpret histograms and optimize statistics for better query performance.

# Chapter 3: Understanding Fragmentation

## 3.1 What is Fragmentation?
- Defining fragmentation in the context of database storage and disk allocation.
- Explaining how fragmentation affects database performance and resource utilization.

## 3.2 Types of Fragmentation:
- Introducing different types of fragmentation, including index fragmentation and file system fragmentation.
- Exploring the causes and consequences of each type of fragmentation in MS SQL Server.

## 3.3 Impact of Fragmentation on Performance:
- Discussing the impact of fragmentation on query performance, disk I/O, and overall system efficiency.
- Exploring how fragmentation can lead to increased resource consumption and degraded user experience.

# Chapter 4: Managing Index Fragmentation

## 4.1 Index Fragmentation Analysis:
- Exploring techniques for analyzing index fragmentation using built-in tools and dynamic management views (DMVs).
- Discussing how to identify fragmented indexes and prioritize them for defragmentation.

## 4.2 Index Reorganization and Rebuilding:
- Discussing the differences between index reorganization and rebuilding and when to use each method.
- Exploring best practices for defragmenting indexes to improve query performance and reduce storage overhead.

## 4.3 Index Maintenance Strategies:
- Providing guidelines for implementing index maintenance tasks as part of a proactive database maintenance plan.
- Discussing techniques for scheduling index maintenance jobs and monitoring their effectiveness.

# Chapter 5: Managing File and Filegroup Fragmentation

## 5.1 File and Filegroup Fragmentation Analysis:

- Exploring techniques for analyzing file and filegroup fragmentation using built-in tools and DMVs.
- Discussing how to identify fragmented files and filegroups and assess their impact on performance.

## 5.2 File Defragmentation and Optimization:

- Discussing strategies for defragmenting files and filegroups to improve disk I/O performance.
- Exploring techniques for optimizing file placement and allocation to minimize fragmentation.

## 5.3 File and Filegroup Maintenance Tasks:

- Providing guidelines for implementing file and filegroup maintenance tasks as part of a comprehensive database maintenance plan.
- Discussing techniques for monitoring file and filegroup fragmentation and automating maintenance tasks.

# Chapter 6: Monitoring and Performance Tuning

## 6.1 Performance Monitoring Tools:

- Introducing performance monitoring tools and utilities for tracking database statistics and fragmentation.
- Exploring built-in tools such as SQL Server Management Studio (SSMS) and third-party monitoring solutions.

## 6.2 Performance Tuning Techniques:

- Discussing performance tuning techniques for optimizing database statistics and fragmentation.
- Exploring strategies for fine-tuning database configurations and resource allocation to mitigate performance issues.

## 6.3 Continuous Improvement:

- Highlighting the importance of continuous monitoring and optimization to maintain peak performance.
- Discussing strategies for establishing performance baselines, analyzing trends, and adapting to changing workload patterns.

# Chapter 7: Real-world Applications and Case Studies

7.1 Database Statistics and Fragmentation Best Practices:

  - Presenting real-world scenarios where database statistics and fragmentation management techniques have been applied to improve performance.

  - Discussing the challenges faced, strategies implemented, and outcomes achieved through effective management.

7.2 Case Studies:

  - Presenting case studies of organizations that have successfully optimized their databases by managing statistics and fragmentation.

  - Exploring the before-and-after performance metrics and the impact of optimization efforts on overall system efficiency.

## Mastering Database Statistics and Fragmentation Management

In summary, mastering database statistics and fragmentation control is important to improve the performance and stability of MS SQL Server for beginners. By understanding the importance of statistical accuracy, performing performance monitoring tasks, and monitoring performance metrics, beginners can improve their SQL skills and complement what is useful in database management. With the knowledge and techniques gained in this comprehensive guide, beginners can confidently manage data statistics and classifications to ensure efficiency and confidence In data centers.

## Enhancing Query Performance: Techniques for Beginners in MS SQL Server

Query performance is an important aspect of database management and affects database performance. Responsiveness and functionality of Microsoft SQL Server (MS SQL)-based applications. As a beginner in the journey of mastering MS SQL, understanding and implementing strategies to improve query performance is crucial to optimizing data and providing insights . In this comprehensive guide, we will review various techniques required for beginners to develop queries in MS SQL Server. From optimizing database design to fine-tuning query execution, this guide is designed to provide beginners with the knowledge and skills they need to properly optimize SQL queries.

# Chapter 1: Efficient Database Design

## 1.1 Normalization:

- Discussing the concept of database normalization and its impact on query performance.
- Exploring normalization levels and best practices for designing well-structured databases to minimize data redundancy and improve query efficiency.

## 1.2 Denormalization:

- Introducing denormalization as a technique for optimizing query performance in certain scenarios.
- Discussing when to denormalize databases and techniques for implementing denormalization effectively while balancing data integrity and performance.

## 1.3 Indexing Strategies:

- Explaining the importance of indexing in optimizing query performance.
- Discussing different types of indexes, such as clustered, non-clustered, and filtered indexes, and their impact on query execution.

# Chapter 2: Writing Efficient Queries

## 2.1 Selecting Necessary Columns:

- Discussing the importance of selecting only the necessary columns in SELECT queries to minimize data retrieval overhead.
- Exploring techniques for avoiding unnecessary columns and calculations in query results.

## 2.2 Optimizing Joins:

- Explaining different join types and their implications for query performance.
- Discussing techniques for optimizing join conditions, order of join operations, and reducing join complexity.

## 2.3 Filtering Data Effectively:

- Introducing techniques for optimizing WHERE clauses to filter data efficiently.
- Exploring the use of indexes, proper data types, and parameterization to improve query performance.

# Chapter 3: Utilizing Indexes for Query Optimization

## 3.1 Understanding Indexing:

- Providing an overview of indexing concepts and their role in query optimization.
- Discussing the benefits of indexing and common pitfalls to avoid.

## 3.2 Choosing the Right Indexes:

- Exploring strategies for selecting appropriate indexes based on query patterns and data access patterns.
- Discussing techniques for evaluating index usage and identifying opportunities for optimization.

## 3.3 Index Maintenance:

- Discussing the importance of index maintenance in preserving query performance over time.
- Exploring techniques for monitoring index health, detecting fragmentation, and performing index maintenance tasks.

# Chapter 4: Query Execution Optimization

## 4.1 Query Plan Analysis:

- Introducing execution plans and their role in optimizing query performance.
- Exploring techniques for analyzing execution plans to identify performance bottlenecks and optimization opportunities.

## 4.2 Query Rewriting and Optimization:

- Discussing strategies for rewriting queries to improve performance, such as restructuring joins and predicates.
- Exploring techniques for optimizing queries for specific use cases and workload patterns.

## 4.3 Parameter Sniffing and Query Plan Caching:

- Explaining parameter sniffing and its impact on query performance.
- Discussing techniques for leveraging query plan caching and plan reuse to improve performance.

# Chapter 5: Performance Monitoring and Tuning

## 5.1 Monitoring Tools and Utilities:

- Introducing performance monitoring tools and utilities available in MS SQL Server.
- Exploring how to use built-in tools such as SQL Server Profiler and Performance Monitor to monitor database performance.

## 5.2 Performance Tuning Techniques:

- Discussing common performance tuning techniques, such as index tuning, query optimization, and server configuration adjustments.
- Exploring strategies for identifying and addressing performance issues in real-time.

## 5.3 Continuous Improvement:

- Highlighting the importance of continuous monitoring and optimization for maintaining optimal performance.
- Discussing strategies for establishing performance baselines, analyzing trends, and adapting to changing workload patterns.

# Chapter 6: Real-world Applications and Case Studies

## 6.1 Query Performance Optimization Best Practices:

- Presenting real-world scenarios where query performance optimization techniques have been applied to improve application performance.
- Discussing the challenges faced, strategies implemented, and outcomes achieved through effective performance tuning.

## 6.2 Case Studies:

- Presenting case studies of organizations that have successfully optimized their queries to achieve significant performance gains.
- Exploring the before-and-after performance metrics and the impact of query optimization on overall system efficiency.

# Mastering Query Performance Optimization

In conclusion, to master query performance optimization, it is important for beginners to know all the capabilities of MS SQL Server. By understanding basic design principles, writing the right questions, using indexing strategies, and executing the right questions, beginners can improve the quality of data and provide better-known information to users. Beginners can confidently optimize SQL queries and contribute to the success of database applications, paper and machines with the knowledge and techniques gained from this comprehensive guide.

# Mastering Stored Procedures: Creation and Usage for Beginners in MS SQL Server

Stored procedures are an integral part of Microsoft's SQL Server (MS SQL) database management system and provide a simple way to encapsulate and execute SQL queries and operations. For those starting to learn MS SQL, understanding how to create and implement stored procedures is crucial to improving the efficiency, manageability and security of database administration. In this comprehensive guide, we'll explore how to create and implement stored procedures in MS SQL Server, giving beginners the knowledge and skills they need to make the most of powerful no.

## Chapter 1: Introduction to Stored Procedures

### 1.1 What are Stored Procedures?
  - Defining stored procedures and their role in database management.
  - Explaining the benefits of using stored procedures, such as code reuse, improved performance, and enhanced security.

### 1.2 Advantages of Stored Procedures:
  - Discussing the advantages of using stored procedures over ad-hoc SQL queries.
  - Exploring how stored procedures promote modularity, simplify maintenance, and enhance database security.

### 1.3 Common Use Cases for Stored Procedures:
  - Presenting common scenarios where stored procedures are beneficial, such as data manipulation, report generation, and business logic implementation.
  - Providing examples of real-world applications of stored procedures in database management.

# Chapter 2: Creating Stored Procedures

## 2.1 Syntax and Structure:

- Introducing the syntax and structure of stored procedures in MS SQL Server.
- Discussing the components of a stored procedure, including the procedure name, parameters, and SQL code.

## 2.2 Parameterized Stored Procedures:

- Explaining the concept of parameterized stored procedures and their advantages in dynamic query execution.
- Demonstrating how to define input and output parameters in stored procedures.

## 2.3 Error Handling and Transactions:

- Discussing techniques for implementing error handling and transactions in stored procedures.
- Exploring best practices for handling errors gracefully and ensuring data integrity in transactional operations.

# Chapter 3: Managing Stored Procedures

## 3.1 Creating and Modifying Stored Procedures:

- Providing step-by-step instructions for creating and modifying stored procedures using SQL Server Management Studio (SSMS) and Transact-SQL (T-SQL).
- Exploring different approaches for managing stored procedures, such as ALTER PROCEDURE and DROP PROCEDURE statements.

## 3.2 Organizing Stored Procedures:

- Discussing strategies for organizing stored procedures within a database structure.
- Exploring techniques for categorizing stored procedures, naming conventions, and documentation best practices.

## 3.3 Version Control and Deployment:

- Introducing version control practices for managing changes to stored procedures.
- Discussing deployment strategies for deploying stored procedures across development, testing, and production environments.

# Chapter 4: Executing Stored Procedures

## 4.1 Invoking Stored Procedures:

- Explaining how to execute stored procedures using SQL Server Management Studio (SSMS), T-SQL scripts, and application code.
- Discussing different methods for invoking stored procedures, such as EXECUTE, EXEC, and sp_executesql.

## 4.2 Passing Parameters:

- Providing examples of passing input and output parameters to stored procedures.
- Exploring techniques for handling optional parameters, default parameter values, and data type conversions.

## 4.3 Result Sets and Output Parameters:

- Explaining how stored procedures can return result sets and output parameters to calling applications.
- Discussing best practices for designing stored procedures to return meaningful results and outputs.


# Chapter 5: Advanced Stored Procedure Concepts

## 5.1 Dynamic SQL:

- Introducing dynamic SQL as a technique for generating and executing SQL statements dynamically within stored procedures.
- Discussing the benefits and risks of dynamic SQL and best practices for its usage.

## 5.2 Nested Stored Procedures:

- Exploring the concept of nested stored procedures and their role in code organization and modularization.
- Discussing considerations for nesting stored procedures and potential performance implications.

## 5.3 Advanced Error Handling:

- Discussing advanced error handling techniques, such as TRY...CATCH blocks and RAISEERROR statements, in stored procedures.
- Exploring how to handle and propagate errors gracefully within nested stored procedures and transactions.

# Chapter 6: Security Considerations

## 6.1 Securing Stored Procedures:

- Discussing security best practices for securing stored procedures and preventing unauthorized access.
- Exploring techniques for implementing role-based access control (RBAC) and granting appropriate permissions to stored procedures.

## 6.2 Parameterized Queries and SQL Injection Prevention:

- Explaining how parameterized queries in stored procedures mitigate the risk of SQL injection attacks.
- Discussing best practices for parameterization and input validation to prevent security vulnerabilities.

## 6.3 Auditing and Logging:

- Exploring techniques for auditing and logging stored procedure execution for security and compliance purposes.
- Discussing the use of SQL Server Audit and Extended Events for capturing and analyzing audit trail data.

# Chapter 7: Real-world Applications and Case Studies

## 7.1 Practical Applications of Stored Procedures:

- Presenting real-world scenarios where stored procedures have been utilized to address specific business requirements.
- Discussing the benefits, challenges, and outcomes of implementing stored procedures in these scenarios.

## 7.2 Case Studies:

- Presenting case studies of organizations that have successfully leveraged stored procedures to improve database performance, security, and maintainability.
- Exploring the before-and-after scenarios and the impact of stored procedure implementations on overall database management.

# Mastering Stored Procedures in MS SQL Server

In summary, knowing stored procedures is very important for beginners to improve MS SQL skills and improve database management. Beginners can leverage these strengths to improve performance, control, and security in MS SQL Server by understanding how to design, implement, and manage storage systems. With the knowledge and skills gained from this comprehensive guide, beginners can confidently use storage systems to solve many database management problems and contribute to the success of information using data and systems.

# Mastering Triggers: Automating Actions Based on Database Events in MS SQL Server

In data management, automatic tracking of database events is a powerful feature that can increase productivity, ensure data accuracy and streamline business processes. Microsoft SQL Server (MS SQL) provides special features called triggers, which are database objects designed to trigger responses to database events. For MS SQL beginners, understanding how to create and use effective values is crucial for daily operations, managing transactions, and maintaining data consistency. In this comprehensive guide, we'll understand the intricacies of triggers and explore their design, use, and best practices. Through practical experience, beginners can improve their SQL skills and unlock the full potential of MS SQL Server automated database operations.

# Chapter 1: Introduction to Triggers

## 1.1 What are Triggers?

   - Defining triggers as database objects that automatically respond to predefined database events.
   - Discussing the role of triggers in automating actions, enforcing business rules, and maintaining data consistency.

## 1.2 Types of Triggers:

   - Introducing different types of triggers supported in MS SQL Server, including DML triggers, DDL triggers, and logon triggers.
   - Exploring the differences between each type of trigger and their respective use cases.

## 1.3 Triggers vs. Stored Procedures:

- Comparing triggers with stored procedures and highlighting the differences in their functionality and usage.
- Discussing scenarios where triggers are more suitable than stored procedures for automating database actions.

# Chapter 2: Creating Triggers

## 2.1 Syntax and Structure:

- Explaining the syntax and structure of trigger creation statements in MS SQL Server.
- Discussing the components of a trigger, including trigger type, triggering event, and trigger body.

## 2.2 Trigger Events:

- Discussing common triggering events, such as INSERT, UPDATE, DELETE, and DDL events, and their significance in trigger execution.
- Exploring how to specify triggering events when creating triggers to automate desired actions.

## 2.3 Trigger Execution Context:

- Explaining the execution context of triggers and how it affects their behavior.
- Discussing the permissions and privileges required for creating and executing triggers in MS SQL Server.

# Chapter 3: Working with DML Triggers

## 3.1 Creating DML Triggers:

- Exploring the creation of DML triggers to automate actions based on data manipulation language (DML) events.
- Discussing use cases for DML triggers, such as auditing changes, enforcing data integrity, and implementing business logic.

## 3.2 Accessing Trigger Data:

- Explaining how to access and manipulate data within DML triggers using the "inserted" and "deleted" logical tables.
- Discussing techniques for using trigger data to enforce business rules and perform conditional actions.

### 3.3 Best Practices for DML Triggers:

- Providing best practices for designing and implementing DML triggers to ensure performance and maintainability.
- Discussing considerations such as trigger logic complexity, transaction management, and error handling.

# Chapter 4: Understanding DDL Triggers

### 4.1 Introduction to DDL Triggers:

- Explaining the concept of data definition language (DDL) triggers and their role in responding to database schema changes.
- Discussing use cases for DDL triggers, such as auditing schema modifications and enforcing database policies.

### 4.2 Creating DDL Triggers:

- Exploring the creation of DDL triggers to capture and respond to schema-level events, such as CREATE, ALTER, and DROP statements.
- Discussing how to define trigger actions and access metadata within DDL triggers.

### 4.3 Limitations and Considerations:

- Discussing limitations and considerations when working with DDL triggers, such as transaction scope and trigger recursion.
- Exploring best practices for designing DDL triggers to minimize performance impact and ensure reliability.

# Chapter 5: Implementing Logon Triggers

### 5.1 Introduction to Logon Triggers:

- Explaining the purpose of logon triggers and their ability to respond to user login events.
- Discussing use cases for logon triggers, such as enforcing security policies and auditing user activity.

### 5.2 Creating Logon Triggers:

- Exploring the creation of logon triggers to perform actions when users connect to the database server.
- Discussing how to define trigger actions and access session information within logon triggers.

## 5.3 Security Considerations:

- Discussing security considerations when implementing logon triggers, such as authentication mechanisms and access control.
- Exploring best practices for designing logon triggers to enhance database security and compliance.

# Chapter 6: Managing and Monitoring Triggers

## 6.1 Altering and Dropping Triggers:

- Explaining how to alter and drop existing triggers in MS SQL Server.
- Discussing considerations for modifying trigger logic and managing trigger dependencies.

## 6.2 Testing and Debugging Triggers:

- Providing techniques for testing and debugging triggers to ensure correct behavior and performance.
- Discussing tools and utilities for tracing trigger execution and diagnosing issues.

## 6.3 Monitoring Trigger Performance:

- Exploring methods for monitoring trigger performance and identifying potential bottlenecks.
- Discussing strategies for optimizing trigger execution and minimizing overhead.

# Chapter 7: Real-world Applications and Case Studies

## 7.1 Trigger Implementation Best Practices:

- Presenting real-world scenarios where triggers have been implemented to automate database actions.
- Discussing the challenges faced, strategies implemented, and outcomes achieved through effective trigger usage.

## 7.2 Case Studies:

- Presenting case studies of organizations that have successfully leveraged triggers to enhance database automation and maintain data integrity.
- Exploring the before-and-after scenarios and the impact of trigger implementation on overall database management.

# Mastering Triggers for Database Automation

In summary, practical knowledge is required for beginners to work with database events and manage data integrity in MS SQL Server. By understanding the nature of competition, creating efficiencies, and applying best practices, startups can use the results to improve business processes, enforce business rules, and advanced database automation. With the knowledge and ideas gained from this comprehensive guide, beginners can confidently use the results to unlock the full capabilities of MS SQL Server and contribute to the success of using database-oriented applications and systems.

# Mastering Transactions: Ensuring Data Integrity in MS SQL Server

In information management, it is important to provide information to maintain its reliability and consistency. Microsoft SQL Server (MS SQL) provides a powerful set of tools, called transactions, that allow developers to group SQL statements into functional requirements and ensure their execution in an atomic and reliable manner. For MS SQL beginners, understanding how business functions work and how to use them is crucial to maintaining data integrity and using robust data sources. In this guide, we will examine the concept of transactions in MS SQL Server, its products, isolation levels, and best practices for ensuring data security. With business knowledge, beginners can improve their SQL skills and create reliable and stable database systems.

## Chapter 1: Introduction to Transactions

### 1.1 Understanding Transactions:

 - Defining transactions as logical units of work that consist of one or more SQL statements.
 - Explaining the properties of transactions, including atomicity, consistency, isolation, and durability (ACID properties).

### 1.2 Benefits of Transactions:

 - Discussing the benefits of using transactions in database applications, such as ensuring data integrity, supporting concurrency control, and facilitating error recovery.

### 1.3 Transaction Control Commands:

 - Introducing transaction control commands in MS SQL Server, including BEGIN TRANSACTION, COMMIT, ROLLBACK, and SAVEPOINT.
 - Explaining how these commands are used to start, commit, rollback, and control the flow of transactions.

# Chapter 2: Managing Transactions in MS SQL Server

## 2.1 Implicit vs. Explicit Transactions:

- Explaining the difference between implicit and explicit transactions in MS SQL Server.
- Discussing when to use each type of transaction and their implications for transaction management.

## 2.2 Nested Transactions:

- Exploring the concept of nested transactions and their behavior within the scope of parent transactions.
- Discussing how nested transactions affect transactional behavior and error handling.

## 2.3 Savepoints:

- Introducing savepoints as a mechanism for defining intermediate points within a transaction.
- Discussing how savepoints can be used to roll back to specific points within a transaction and handle complex error scenarios.

# Chapter 3: Transaction Isolation Levels

## 3.1 Understanding Isolation Levels:

- Introducing transaction isolation levels and their role in controlling the visibility of data changes within transactions.
- Explaining the different isolation levels supported by MS SQL Server, including READ UNCOMMITTED, READ COMMITTED, REPEATABLE READ, and SERIALIZABLE.

## 3.2 Isolation Level Considerations:

- Discussing the trade-offs associated with each isolation level in terms of concurrency, consistency, and performance.
- Exploring scenarios where different isolation levels are appropriate based on application requirements and data access patterns.

## 3.3 Setting Isolation Levels:

- Explaining how to set transaction isolation levels in MS SQL Server using transaction isolation level statements or database connection options.
- Discussing best practices for choosing and configuring isolation levels to ensure the desired balance between performance and data consistency.

# Chapter 4: Best Practices for Transaction Management

## 4.1 Transaction Design Considerations:

- Discussing best practices for designing transactions to ensure data integrity and minimize concurrency issues.
- Exploring techniques for breaking down complex operations into smaller, more manageable transactions.

## 4.2 Error Handling and Rollback Strategies:

- Explaining strategies for handling errors within transactions and rolling back changes in case of exceptions.
- Discussing the use of try-catch blocks and transaction savepoints for implementing robust error handling mechanisms.

## 4.3 Optimizing Transaction Performance:

- Providing tips and techniques for optimizing transaction performance in MS SQL Server.
- Discussing strategies for reducing transaction overhead, minimizing locking contention, and improving throughput.

# Chapter 5: Advanced Transaction Topics

## 5.1 Distributed Transactions:

- Introducing distributed transactions and their role in coordinating transactions across multiple databases or systems.
- Discussing techniques for implementing distributed transactions using distributed transaction coordinators (DTC) and two-phase commit protocols.

## 5.2 Snapshot Isolation:

- Exploring snapshot isolation as an alternative isolation level for providing consistent query results without blocking.
- Discussing the benefits and limitations of snapshot isolation and how to enable it in MS SQL Server databases.

## 5.3 Transaction Log Management:

- Discussing the importance of transaction logs in maintaining data durability and supporting transaction recovery.
- Exploring techniques for managing transaction logs, such as backing up transaction logs, monitoring log growth, and optimizing log file placement.

# Chapter 6: Real-world Applications and Case Studies

## 6.1 Transaction Management Best Practices:

- Presenting real-world scenarios where transaction management techniques have been applied to ensure data integrity and reliability.
- Discussing the challenges faced, strategies implemented, and outcomes achieved through effective transaction management.

## 6.2 Case Studies:

- Presenting case studies of organizations that have successfully implemented transactions to maintain data integrity and support business-critical applications.
- Exploring the before-and-after scenarios and the impact of transaction management on overall system reliability and performance.

# Mastering Transactions for Data Integrity

In summary, business knowledge is required for beginners to ensure the integrity and reliability of data in MS SQL Server. Beginners can create effective and efficient data sources by understanding the basics of business management, choosing appropriate separation levels and applying practices: best for errors and good work. With the knowledge and techniques gained in this comprehensive guide, beginners can confidently implement changes to maintain data integrity and support business-critical MS SQL Server.

# Mastering Common Table Expressions (CTEs) and Window Functions in MS SQL Server

In the world of data management, multiple instructions (CTEs) and task windows are powerful features that allow developers to write more difficult and interesting questions. Microsoft SQL Server (MS SQL) provides maximum capability for data management, collection and analysis by providing strong support for CTE and task windows. For MS SQL beginners, understanding how to use CTEs and window functions is crucial to writing concise, readable and efficient content. In this comprehensive guide, we'll understand the differences between CTEs and task windows and review their syntax, usage, and best practices. Beginners can improve their SQL skills by learning CTE and Windows functions and unlock the full capabilities of MS SQL Server for data analysis and reporting.

# Chapter 1: Introduction to Common Table Expressions (CTEs)

## 1.1 Understanding CTEs:

- Defining Common Table Expressions (CTEs) as temporary result sets that can be referenced within a SELECT, INSERT, UPDATE, or DELETE statement.
- Explaining the benefits of using CTEs, such as improving query readability, modularizing complex queries, and enhancing performance.

## 1.2 Syntax and Structure:

- Explaining the syntax and structure of CTEs in MS SQL Server, including the WITH clause and the recursive CTEs.
- Discussing the components of a CTE, such as the anchor member, recursive member (if applicable), and the final SELECT statement.

## 1.3 Recursive CTEs:

- Introducing recursive CTEs as a special type of CTE used to query hierarchical or recursive data structures.
- Exploring recursive CTE syntax, common use cases, and best practices for writing efficient recursive queries.

# Chapter 2: Working with Common Table Expressions (CTEs)

## 2.1 CTE Usage Scenarios:

- Discussing common scenarios where CTEs are useful, such as hierarchical data querying, recursive data processing, and self-referencing table operations.
- Providing real-world examples and use cases to illustrate the practical applications of CTEs in MS SQL Server.

## 2.2 CTE Performance Considerations:

- Exploring performance considerations when using CTEs in queries, such as query optimization, index usage, and query plan analysis.
- Discussing techniques for optimizing CTE queries and minimizing performance overhead.

## 2.3 Nesting CTEs:

- Discussing the ability to nest CTEs within other CTEs or query expressions to achieve more complex query logic.
- Providing guidelines for nesting CTEs effectively while maintaining query readability and performance.

# Chapter 3: Introduction to Window Functions

## 3.1 Understanding Window Functions:

- Defining window functions as a category of SQL functions that operate on a subset of rows defined by a window or partition.
- Explaining the benefits of using window functions for data aggregation, ranking, and analytical processing.

## 3.2 Syntax and Usage:

- Exploring the syntax and usage of window functions in MS SQL Server, including the OVER clause and the various window function types.
- Discussing common window function types, such as aggregate functions, ranking functions, and analytic functions.

## 3.3 Window Partitioning:

- Explaining the concept of window partitioning and how it defines the groups of rows over which window functions operate.
- Discussing techniques for partitioning data using the PARTITION BY clause and controlling window frame boundaries.

# Chapter 4: Working with Window Functions

## 4.1 Aggregate Window Functions:

- Discussing aggregate window functions, such as SUM(), AVG(), MIN(), and MAX(), and their usage for computing summary statistics over window partitions.
- Providing examples of aggregate window functions in practical scenarios, such as calculating running totals and averages.

## 4.2 Ranking Window Functions:

- Exploring ranking window functions, including ROW_NUMBER(), RANK(), DENSE_RANK(), and NTILE(), and their applications for assigning rankings to rows within window partitions.
- Discussing use cases for ranking window functions, such as pagination, top-N queries, and data deduplication.

## 4.3 Analytic Window Functions:

- Discussing analytic window functions, such as LAG(), LEAD(), FIRST_VALUE(), and LAST_VALUE(), and their usage for performing analytical calculations based on neighboring rows within window partitions.

- Providing examples of analytic window functions in scenarios such as time-series analysis, trend detection, and data interpolation.

# Chapter 5: Advanced Topics in CTEs and Window Functions

### 5.1 Recursive CTEs with Window Functions:

- Exploring advanced techniques for combining recursive CTEs with window functions to solve complex analytical problems.
- Discussing practical applications of recursive CTEs with window functions, such as hierarchical data aggregation and graph traversal.

### 5.2 Performance Optimization Strategies:

- Providing advanced tips and techniques for optimizing CTEs and window functions to improve query performance.
- Discussing considerations such as index usage, query rewriting, and query plan analysis for optimizing complex queries.

### 5.3 Error Handling and Debugging:

- Discussing strategies for error handling and debugging when working with CTEs and window functions.
- Exploring techniques for troubleshooting common issues, such as incorrect results, performance bottlenecks, and syntax errors.

# Chapter 6: Real-world Applications and Case Studies

### 6.1 CTEs and Window Functions in Practice:

- Presenting real-world scenarios where CTEs and window functions have been applied to solve complex analytical challenges.
- Discussing the challenges faced, strategies implemented, and outcomes achieved through the effective use of CTEs and window functions.

### 6.2 Case Studies:

- Presenting case studies of organizations that have successfully leveraged CTEs and window functions to gain insights from their data.
- Exploring the before-and-after scenarios and the impact of CTEs and window functions on decision-making and business intelligence.

# Mastering CTEs and Window Functions for Advanced SQL Analysis

As a result, mastering common table expressions (CTEs) and window functions is important for beginners to perform advanced SQL analysis and derive insights from data in MS SQL Server. By understanding the syntax, usage, and best practices of CTE and window functions, beginners can write effective queries and presentations, manage data effectively, and unlock the full capabilities of MS SQL Server for data analysis and reporting. . With the knowledge and techniques gained in this comprehensive guide, beginners can confidently use CTE and window functionality to solve complex analysis problems and provide effective solutions to their information.

# Navigating Error Handling: Strategies for Handling Exceptions and Errors in MS SQL Server

In the dynamic world of database management, errors and exceptions are inevitable. Whether due to incorrect data entry, failure to fulfill a requirement, or operational error, handling exceptions and errors effectively is important to ensure fair data management, ensure application reliability, and provide a good user experience. Microsoft SQL Server (MS SQL) provides a powerful set of features and techniques for handling errors and exceptions, allowing developers to predict, execute, and recover from unexpected events. For those new to MS SQL, understanding how to handle errors effectively is crucial to building effective databases. In this comprehensive guide, we will review various techniques and best practices for handling exceptions and errors in MS SQL Server. By learning from mistakes, beginners can improve their SQL skills and create powerful and reliable database systems.

# Chapter 1: Introduction to Error Handling in MS SQL Server

## 1.1 Understanding Errors and Exceptions:

  - Defining errors and exceptions in the context of database management and application development.
  - Explaining common sources of errors, such as programming mistakes, invalid data inputs, and system failures.

## 1.2 Importance of Error Handling:

  - Discussing the significance of error handling in maintaining data integrity, ensuring application reliability, and providing a seamless user experience.
  - Exploring the impact of unhandled errors on application performance, security, and user satisfaction.

### 1.3 Error Handling Mechanisms in MS SQL Server:

- Introducing error handling mechanisms provided by MS SQL Server, including try-catch blocks, error functions, and system views.
- Explaining how these mechanisms enable developers to detect, handle, and recover from errors effectively.

## Chapter 2: Using Try-Catch Blocks for Error Handling

### 2.1 Syntax and Structure of Try-Catch Blocks:

- Explaining the syntax and structure of try-catch blocks in MS SQL Server.
- Discussing how try-catch blocks allow developers to encapsulate error-prone code and handle exceptions gracefully.

### 2.2 Error Handling with Try-Catch Blocks:

- Exploring the role of try-catch blocks in detecting and handling errors during query execution.
- Discussing best practices for writing robust try-catch blocks, such as logging error details and providing meaningful error messages.

### 2.3 Nesting Try-Catch Blocks:

- Discussing the ability to nest try-catch blocks within other try-catch blocks to handle errors at different levels of code execution.
- Exploring scenarios where nested try-catch blocks are useful and discussing considerations for error propagation and handling.

## Chapter 3: Using Error Functions and System Views

### 3.1 Error Functions:

- Introducing error functions provided by MS SQL Server, such as ERROR_MESSAGE(), ERROR_NUMBER(), ERROR_STATE(), and ERROR_LINE().
- Explaining how error functions can be used within try-catch blocks to retrieve information about the error condition.

### 3.2 System Views for Error Logging:

- Exploring system views in MS SQL Server, such as sys.messages and sys.dm_exec_requests, for monitoring and logging error information.
- Discussing techniques for querying system views to analyze error trends, diagnose performance issues, and track application errors.

### 3.3 Custom Error Handling:

- Discussing the implementation of custom error handling solutions using error functions and system views.
- Exploring techniques for logging errors to custom tables, sending email alerts, and triggering automated responses based on error conditions.

# Chapter 4: Transaction Error Handling

### 4.1 Error Handling in Transactions:

- Explaining how errors are handled within transactional contexts in MS SQL Server.
- Discussing the behavior of transactions in the presence of errors and the mechanisms for rolling back transactions to ensure data integrity.

### 4.2 Managing Transaction Rollbacks:

- Exploring strategies for managing transaction rollbacks effectively to handle errors and maintain data consistency.
- Discussing techniques for implementing conditional transaction rollbacks based on error conditions and application logic.

### 4.3 Savepoints and Error Recovery:

- Introducing savepoints as a mechanism for defining intermediate points within a transaction for error recovery.
- Discussing how savepoints can be used to roll back to specific points within a transaction and handle errors gracefully.

# Chapter 5: Error Handling Best Practices

### 5.1 Defensive Programming Techniques:

- Discussing defensive programming techniques for preventing errors and handling unexpected situations proactively.
- Exploring practices such as input validation, error checking, and exception handling to enhance code robustness and reliability.

### 5.2 Logging and Monitoring:

- Highlighting the importance of logging and monitoring in error handling for diagnosing issues, tracking error trends, and ensuring system reliability.
- Discussing best practices for implementing comprehensive logging and monitoring solutions using built-in features and third-party tools.

## 5.3 Continuous Improvement:

- Discussing the importance of continuous improvement in error handling through code reviews, error analysis, and feedback mechanisms.
- Exploring strategies for identifying and addressing recurring errors, enhancing error messages, and optimizing error handling logic.

# Chapter 6: Real-world Applications and Case Studies

## 6.1 Error Handling in Practice:

- Presenting real-world scenarios where effective error handling techniques have been applied to solve complex problems and maintain application reliability.
- Discussing the challenges faced, strategies implemented, and outcomes achieved through the use of error handling mechanisms.

## 6.2 Case Studies:

- Presenting case studies of organizations that have successfully implemented error handling solutions in MS SQL Server.
- Exploring the before-and-after scenarios and the impact of error handling on application performance, data integrity, and user satisfaction.

# Mastering Error Handling for Robust Database Applications

Mastering error handling is crucial for ensuring the robustness of database applications. Implementing comprehensive error handling mechanisms helps in identifying, logging, and gracefully managing errors that may arise during database operations. This involves anticipating potential issues such as connection failures, query errors, or data integrity violations, and implementing strategies to handle them effectively. Techniques such as structured exception handling, error logging, retry mechanisms, and graceful degradation can significantly enhance the reliability and resilience of database applications. By mastering error handling, developers can improve the user experience, prevent data loss, and maintain the overall stability of their applications in the face of unexpected challenges.

# Mastering User Roles and Permissions in MS SQL Server

Using user permissions in the field of data management is an important factor in ensuring data security, fairness and compliance with the rules. Microsoft SQL Server (MS SQL) provides a powerful mechanism for managing user access and permissions, allowing administrators to define the right permissions to control user activity on information. For MS SQL beginners, understanding how to implement user roles and permissions is crucial to controlling access to sensitive data and preventing unauthorized (valid or modified) access. In this guide, we'll explore the intricacies of user roles and permissions in MS SQL Server, best practices for protecting database information, including topics like role management, permission types, and methods. Beginners can improve their SQL skills and create secure and scalable database systems by knowing user roles and permissions.

# Chapter 1: Introduction to User Roles and Permissions

## 1.1 Understanding User Roles:

  - Defining user roles as collections of permissions or privileges assigned to users or groups of users.
  - Explaining the benefits of using user roles for managing access control, simplifying permission management, and enforcing security policies.

## 1.2 Importance of Permissions:

  - Discussing the significance of permissions in controlling user actions within the database, such as querying, inserting, updating, and deleting data.
  - Exploring the implications of granting appropriate permissions to users based on their roles and responsibilities.

## 1.3 Regulatory Compliance:

  - Highlighting the importance of maintaining compliance with regulatory requirements, such as GDPR, HIPAA, and SOX, through effective user access control and permissions management.
  - Discussing how role-based access control (RBAC) helps organizations achieve compliance with data protection regulations.

# Chapter 2: Managing User Roles in MS SQL Server

## 2.1 Role-Based Access Control (RBAC):

- Explaining the concept of Role-Based Access Control (RBAC) and its role in defining access permissions based on user roles.
- Discussing the advantages of RBAC, such as centralized access management, scalability, and ease of maintenance.

## 2.2 Built-in Database Roles:

- Introducing built-in database roles provided by MS SQL Server, such as db_owner, db_datareader, and db_datawriter, and their default permissions.
- Exploring the purpose of each built-in role and its implications for user access control.

## 2.3 Custom Database Roles:

- Discussing the creation of custom database roles tailored to specific business requirements and access control policies.
- Providing guidelines for creating and managing custom roles, including assigning permissions and adding members.

# Chapter 3: Granting and Revoking Permissions

## 3.1 Types of Permissions:

- Explaining the different types of permissions in MS SQL Server, including object-level permissions, statement-level permissions, and schema-level permissions.
- Discussing how each type of permission controls access to database objects and operations.

## 3.2 Granting Permissions:

- Discussing the GRANT statement in MS SQL Server and its role in assigning permissions to users or roles.
- Explaining how to grant specific permissions, such as SELECT, INSERT, UPDATE, DELETE, EXECUTE, and REFERENCES, on database objects.

## 3.3 Revoking Permissions:

- Exploring the REVOKE statement and its usage for removing previously granted permissions from users or roles.
- Discussing best practices for revoking permissions to ensure data security and compliance with access control policies.

# Chapter 4: Securing Database Objects

## 4.1 Securing Tables and Views:

- Discussing strategies for securing tables and views in MS SQL Server to prevent unauthorized access or modifications.
- Exploring techniques such as granting selective permissions, implementing row-level security, and encrypting sensitive data.

## 4.2 Securing Stored Procedures and Functions:

- Exploring best practices for securing stored procedures and functions to control access to business logic and data manipulation operations.
- Discussing permission requirements for executing stored procedures and functions, and techniques for restricting access to sensitive procedures.

## 4.3 Securing Database Schema:

- Discussing the importance of securing the database schema to protect against unauthorized changes to database structures.
- Exploring techniques such as schema ownership chaining, schema-level permissions, and schema binding to enforce data integrity and security.


# Chapter 5: Implementing Row-Level Security

## 5.1 Row-Level Security (RLS):

- Introducing Row-Level Security (RLS) as a feature in MS SQL Server for controlling access to rows within a table based on user permissions.
- Explaining the benefits of RLS in scenarios where users should only have access to specific rows based on their roles or attributes.

## 5.2 Policy-Based Access Control:

- Discussing how to implement policy-based access control using RLS policies to define row-level security predicates.
- Exploring practical use cases for RLS, such as multi-tenant applications, data partitioning, and compliance with privacy regulations.

# Chapter 6: Auditing and Monitoring User Access

## 6.1 Audit Logging:

- Explaining the importance of audit logging for tracking user access and monitoring database activity.
- Discussing how to implement audit logging in MS SQL Server using features such as SQL Server Audit and Extended Events.

## 6.2 Monitoring User Activity:

- Discussing techniques for monitoring user activity and detecting unauthorized access or suspicious behavior.
- Exploring tools and utilities for monitoring user sessions, query execution, and database changes in real-time.

# Chapter 7: Real-world Applications and Case Studies

## 7.1 Role-Based Access Control in Practice:

- Presenting real-world scenarios where role-based access control has been implemented to secure database resources and enforce access policies.
- Discussing the challenges faced, strategies implemented, and outcomes achieved through effective role-based access control.

## 7.2 Case Studies:

- Presenting case studies of organizations that have successfully implemented user roles and permissions to achieve data security and compliance goals.
- Exploring the before-and-after scenarios and the impact of role-based access control on data protection and regulatory compliance.

## Mastering User Roles and Permissions for Data Security

In summary, it is important for beginners to know user roles and permissions to ensure data security, integrity, and compliance with MS SQL Server standards. By understanding the basics of managing access to roles, using the right permissions, and monitoring clients, beginners can create a secure environment and keep track of information. With the knowledge and ideas gained from this comprehensive guide, beginners can confidently use user roles and permissions to protect sensitive data, protect the inaccessible, and reduce security risks in MS SQL Server environments.

# Mastering Backup and Restore Strategies in MS SQL Server

Database management and implementation of a strong backup and recovery strategy is crucial to protecting data from loss, corruption and unexpected damage. Microsoft SQL Server (MS SQL) provides a comprehensive set of tools and features for backup and recovery, allowing administrators to protect critical data and minimize downtime during downtime. For MS SQL beginners, understanding backup and recovery strategies is crucial to ensuring data reliability, operational continuity, and regulatory compliance. In this comprehensive guide, we'll explore the intricacies of the backup and recovery process in MS SQL Server, including topics such as backup types, backup models, backup schedules, and best practices. Beginners can improve their SQL skills and create secure and reliable database systems by learning backup and recovery techniques.

# Chapter 1: Introduction to Backup and Restore Concepts

## 1.1 Importance of Backup and Restore:

- Defining backup and restore as essential processes for protecting data integrity, ensuring business continuity, and mitigating risks of data loss.
- Explaining the consequences of data loss or corruption and the importance of implementing reliable backup and restore strategies.

## 1.2 Backup Types:

- Introducing different types of backups supported in MS SQL Server, including full backups, differential backups, and transaction log backups.
- Explaining the purpose and characteristics of each backup type and their role in comprehensive data protection.

## 1.3 Recovery Models:

- Discussing the three recovery models supported in MS SQL Server: Simple, Full, and Bulk-Logged.
- Explaining the differences between recovery models and their implications for backup and restore operations.

# Chapter 2: Planning Backup and Restore Strategies

## 2.1 Data Backup Requirements:

- Discussing factors to consider when planning backup strategies, such as data criticality, recovery objectives, and regulatory compliance.
- Exploring techniques for identifying data backup requirements based on business needs and risk assessments.

## 2.2 Backup Storage Considerations:

- Explaining considerations for selecting backup storage options, such as disk storage, tape storage, and cloud storage.
- Discussing best practices for ensuring data security, durability, and accessibility when storing backups.

## 2.3 Backup Retention Policies:

- Introducing backup retention policies and their role in managing backup sets over time.
- Discussing factors to consider when defining backup retention periods, such as compliance requirements and storage constraints.

# Chapter 3: Performing Database Backups

## 3.1 Full Database Backups:

- Explaining how to perform full database backups in MS SQL Server using SQL Server Management Studio (SSMS) or Transact-SQL (T-SQL) commands.
- Providing step-by-step instructions for creating full database backups and verifying their completion.

## 3.2 Differential Backups:

- Discussing the concept of differential backups and their role in reducing backup times and storage requirements.
- Explaining how to schedule and perform differential backups to capture changes since the last full backup.

## 3.3 Transaction Log Backups:

- Exploring transaction log backups and their importance for maintaining transactional consistency and enabling point-in-time recovery.
- Providing guidance on scheduling and managing transaction log backups to minimize data loss in case of failure.

# Chapter 4: Automating Backup Operations

## 4.1 Backup Scheduling:

- Discussing strategies for automating backup operations using SQL Server Agent jobs and Maintenance Plans.
- Explaining how to create and schedule backup jobs to run at regular intervals and ensure data protection without manual intervention.

## 4.2 Backup Verification:

- Exploring techniques for verifying the integrity and completeness of backup sets, such as backup checksums and restore testing.
- Discussing the importance of regular backup verification to ensure data recoverability and identify potential issues early.

## 4.3 Monitoring Backup Performance:

- Discussing methods for monitoring backup performance and identifying potential bottlenecks or failures.
- Exploring built-in tools and third-party utilities for tracking backup progress, analyzing backup history, and troubleshooting issues.

# Chapter 5: Database Restore Strategies

## 5.1 Point-in-Time Recovery:

- Explaining the concept of point-in-time recovery (PITR) and its importance for recovering databases to specific moments in time.
- Discussing how to perform point-in-time recovery using full backups, differential backups, and transaction log backups.

## 5.2 Complete Database Restore:

- Providing step-by-step instructions for performing complete database restores from full backups, including considerations for recovery models and backup chains.
- Exploring scenarios where complete database restores are necessary, such as disaster recovery or database migration.

## 5.3 Partial Database Restore:

- Discussing partial database restores and their applications for recovering specific filegroups or database objects.
- Explaining how to perform partial restores using file backups or piecemeal restores to minimize downtime and data loss.

# Chapter 6: Disaster Recovery Planning

## 6.1 Disaster Recovery Strategies:

- Discussing disaster recovery strategies and their role in mitigating the impact of catastrophic events on database operations.
- Exploring techniques such as geo-replication, failover clustering, and database mirroring for achieving high availability and disaster recovery.

## 6.2 Backup Offsite Storage:

- Exploring the importance of offsite backup storage for disaster recovery preparedness.
- Discussing strategies for replicating backups to offsite locations, such as cloud storage or remote data centers, to ensure data availability in case of local failures.

## 6.3 Backup and Restore Testing:

- Discussing the importance of backup and restore testing in validating disaster recovery plans and procedures.
- Exploring techniques for conducting backup and restore drills, simulating disaster scenarios, and evaluating recovery readiness.

# Chapter 7: Real-world Applications and Case Studies

## 7.1 Backup and Restore Best Practices:

- Presenting real-world scenarios where backup and restore strategies have been applied to protect against data loss and ensure business continuity.
- Discussing the challenges faced, strategies implemented, and outcomes achieved through effective backup and restore practices.

## 7.2 Case Studies:

- Presenting case studies of organizations that have successfully implemented backup and restore strategies to recover from data loss or disasters.
- Exploring the before-and-after scenarios and the impact of backup and restore strategies on business operations and customer trust.

# Mastering Backup and Restore for Data Resilience

In summary, knowledge of backup and recovery strategies is essential for beginners to protect their data from loss, corruption and damage in MS SQL Server at every turn. Beginners can create a safe and reliable database system by understanding backup types, scheduling backups, performing regular backups, and testing recovery procedures. With the knowledge and techniques gained in this comprehensive guide, beginners can confidently use backup and recovery techniques to protect important data, ensure the continued operation of businesses, and reduce risks in MS SQL Server environments.

# Mastering Database Health and Performance Monitoring in MS SQL Server

Managing and monitoring the health and employment information in the record is important in ensuring effective performance, identifying problems that may arise, and maintaining interest and performance. Microsoft SQL Server (MS SQL) provides tools and features to monitor data health and performance, allowing administrators to monitor resource usage, control bottlenecks, and increase efficiency. For those new to MS SQL, understanding how to monitor data health and performance is crucial to identifying and resolving problems and ensuring the reliability and performance of database operations. In this comprehensive guide, we'll explore the intricacies of data health and performance monitoring in MS SQL Server, including topics such as performance visualization, efficiency, querying and monitoring, and best practices for troubleshooting. Beginners can improve their SQL skills and create powerful and responsive databases by learning database management techniques.

# Chapter 1: Introduction to Database Monitoring

## 1.1 Importance of Database Monitoring:

  - Defining database monitoring as the process of tracking database health, performance metrics, and resource utilization.
  - Explaining the importance of database monitoring for identifying performance bottlenecks, optimizing resource usage, and ensuring system reliability.

## 1.2 Key Metrics for Monitoring:

  - Discussing essential metrics for monitoring database health and performance, including CPU usage, memory usage, disk I/O, and query execution times.
  - Exploring how these metrics provide insights into system health, resource contention, and workload patterns.

## 1.3 Monitoring Tools and Techniques:

- Introducing built-in monitoring tools and techniques available in MS SQL Server, such as Dynamic Management Views (DMVs), Performance Monitor, and SQL Server Profiler.
- Discussing third-party monitoring solutions and their capabilities for advanced performance analysis and troubleshooting.

# Chapter 2: Dynamic Management Views (DMVs)

## 2.1 Understanding DMVs:

- Explaining Dynamic Management Views (DMVs) as a set of system views and functions that provide real-time insights into database performance and resource usage.
- Introducing commonly used DMVs for monitoring aspects such as CPU utilization, memory usage, disk activity, and query execution statistics.

## 2.2 Querying DMVs:

- Discussing techniques for querying DMVs to retrieve performance metrics and diagnostic information.
- Providing examples of SQL queries that leverage DMVs to monitor database health and performance in real-time.

## 2.3 Interpreting DMV Results:

- Exploring how to interpret and analyze the results obtained from DMV queries.
- Discussing common performance issues and their indicators in DMV data, such as high CPU usage, memory pressure, and disk latency.

# Chapter 3: Performance Counters and Metrics

## 3.1 Introduction to Performance Counters:

- Introducing Performance Monitor (PerfMon) and its role in monitoring system performance using performance counters.
- Explaining how to use PerfMon to track key performance metrics, such as CPU usage, memory utilization, disk activity, and network throughput.

## 3.2 Important Performance Metrics:

- Discussing essential performance counters and metrics for monitoring database health and performance.
- Exploring how performance counters provide insights into system resource utilization, query execution times, and database throughput.

### 3.3 Customizing Performance Counters:

- Exploring techniques for customizing PerfMon to track specific performance metrics and counters relevant to database workloads.
- Discussing best practices for selecting and configuring performance counters based on monitoring requirements and performance goals.

## Chapter 4: Query Tuning and Optimization

### 4.1 Identifying Performance Bottlenecks:

- Discussing common performance bottlenecks in database systems, such as CPU contention, memory pressure, disk I/O latency, and query inefficiencies.
- Exploring techniques for identifying and diagnosing performance issues using monitoring tools and performance analysis.

### 4.2 Query Execution Analysis:

- Introducing SQL Server Profiler and its role in capturing and analyzing query execution events.
- Discussing how to use SQL Server Profiler to identify slow-running queries, excessive resource consumption, and inefficient query execution plans.

### 4.3 Query Tuning Strategies:

- Exploring query tuning strategies for optimizing query performance and improving database throughput.
- Discussing techniques such as index optimization, query rewriting, parameterization, and statistics management for improving query execution efficiency.

## Chapter 5: Proactive Monitoring and Alerting

### 5.1 Setting Up Alerts:

- Discussing the importance of proactive monitoring and alerting for detecting and responding to performance issues in real-time.
- Exploring how to configure alerts based on predefined thresholds or performance conditions using SQL Server Agent and Database Mail.

### 5.2 Performance Baselines:

- Explaining the concept of performance baselines and their role in establishing normal operating conditions for database systems.
- Discussing techniques for capturing and analyzing performance baselines to detect deviations and anomalies.

## 5.3 Automated Remediation:

- Introducing automated remediation techniques for addressing performance issues and optimizing system resources.
- Discussing the use of automation scripts, policies, and maintenance tasks for proactive performance management and optimization.

# Chapter 6: Best Practices for Database Monitoring

## 6.1 Regular Health Checks:

- Discussing the importance of conducting regular health checks and performance audits to assess database health and identify potential issues.
- Exploring best practices for performing health checks, analyzing performance trends, and addressing emerging issues proactively.

## 6.2 Capacity Planning:

- Introducing capacity planning as a proactive approach to anticipating future resource requirements and scaling database infrastructure accordingly.
- Discussing techniques for estimating resource needs, forecasting growth, and planning for scalability and performance optimization.

## 6.3 Continuous Improvement:

- Discussing the importance of continuous improvement in database monitoring and performance management.
- Exploring strategies for implementing feedback loops, reviewing performance metrics, and refining monitoring processes to optimize database operations over time.

# Chapter 7: Real-world Applications and Case Studies

## 7.1 Monitoring Best Practices in Action:

- Presenting real-world scenarios where database monitoring best practices have been applied to optimize performance, detect issues, and ensure system reliability.
- Discussing the challenges faced, strategies implemented, and outcomes achieved through effective monitoring practices.

## 7.2 Case Studies:

- Presenting case studies of organizations that have successfully implemented database monitoring solutions to improve performance and reliability.
- Exploring the before-and-after scenarios and the impact of monitoring strategies on business operations and customer satisfaction.

# Essential Maintenance Tasks: Index Rebuilds and Statistics Updates in MS SQL Server

Continuous maintenance work is essential. Performance and stability of your Microsoft SQL Server (MS SQL) database. Among these activities, innovation and statistical updates play an important role in improving query performance, increasing database efficiency, and reducing resource contention. For those new to MS SQL, understanding the importance of tracking metrics and identifying updates and learning how to perform these tasks effectively is the key to effective database management. In this comprehensive guide, we will explore the importance of business development and statistical updates in MS SQL Server, discuss best practices for performing maintenance tasks, and provide recommendations for improving data through continuous monitoring.

## Chapter 1: Understanding Indexes and Statistics

1.1 Introduction to Indexes:

  - Define indexes in MS SQL Server as data structures that enhance query performance by facilitating efficient data retrieval.
  - Explain the different types of indexes, including clustered and non-clustered indexes, and their impact on query execution.

1.2 Importance of Statistics:

  - Discuss the role of statistics in query optimization and execution plan generation.
  - Explain how statistics help the query optimizer make informed decisions about query execution paths.

## Chapter 2: Index Rebuilds: Concepts and Best Practices

2.1 Index Fragmentation:

  - Define index fragmentation and its impact on query performance.
  - Discuss the types of fragmentation, including logical and physical fragmentation, and their causes.

2.2 Index Maintenance Strategies:

  - Explore various strategies for index maintenance, including index rebuilds and index reorganization.
  - Discuss the advantages and disadvantages of each strategy and when to use them.

## 2.3 Best Practices for Index Rebuilds:

- Provide guidelines for scheduling and performing index rebuilds in MS SQL Server.
- Discuss factors to consider, such as index fragmentation levels, database activity, and maintenance windows.

# Chapter 3: Statistics Updates: Concepts and Best Practices

## 3.1 Understanding Statistics:

- Explain the purpose of statistics in MS SQL Server and how they influence query optimization.
- Discuss the components of statistics, including histogram and density values.

## 3.2 Automatic Statistics Updates:

- Discuss how MS SQL Server automatically updates statistics to maintain query performance.
- Explain the threshold for automatic statistics updates and the factors that trigger updates.

## 3.3 Manual Statistics Updates:

- Provide guidance on when to perform manual statistics updates and how to do so using the UPDATE STATISTICS statement.
- Discuss scenarios where manual updates are necessary, such as after bulk data modifications or database maintenance.

# Chapter 4: Monitoring and Maintaining Indexes and Statistics

## 4.1 Index and Statistics Views:

- Introduce Dynamic Management Views (DMVs) and system catalog views for monitoring indexes and statistics.
- Discuss the information provided by these views and how to interpret it.

## 4.2 Performance Monitoring:

- Explain how to use performance monitoring tools, such as SQL Server Profiler and Performance Monitor, to monitor index and statistics performance.
- Discuss key performance metrics to monitor, such as index fragmentation levels and query execution times.

### 4.3 Alerting and Notifications:

- Discuss the importance of setting up alerts and notifications for index and statistics maintenance.
- Provide guidance on configuring alerts for conditions such as high index fragmentation or outdated statistics.

# Chapter 5: Advanced Techniques for Index and Statistics Maintenance

### 5.1 Partitioned Tables and Indexes:

- Explain how partitioning affects index and statistics maintenance.
- Discuss strategies for managing indexes and statistics on partitioned tables effectively.

### 5.2 Online Index Operations:

- Discuss the benefits of performing index maintenance operations online to minimize downtime.
- Explain how to perform online index rebuilds and statistics updates in MS SQL Server.

### 5.3 Index and Statistics Maintenance Plans:

- Introduce Maintenance Plans in MS SQL Server for automating index and statistics maintenance tasks.
- Provide guidance on creating and scheduling Maintenance Plans to ensure regular maintenance.

# Chapter 6: Best Practices and Common Pitfalls

### 6.1 Best Practices for Index Maintenance:

- Summarize best practices for index maintenance, including regular monitoring, proactive maintenance, and careful scheduling.
- Discuss common pitfalls to avoid, such as over-indexing and neglecting index maintenance.

### 6.2 Best Practices for Statistics Updates:

- Summarize best practices for statistics updates, including regular monitoring, targeted updates, and automation.
- Discuss common pitfalls to avoid, such as relying solely on automatic updates and ignoring outdated statistics.

# Chapter 7: Real-world Scenarios and Case Studies

## 7.1 Real-world Scenarios:

- Present real-world scenarios where effective index maintenance and statistics updates have improved query performance and database efficiency.
- Discuss the challenges faced, solutions implemented, and outcomes achieved in each scenario.

## 7.2 Case Studies:

- Present case studies of organizations that have successfully implemented index maintenance and statistics update strategies.
- Explore the impact of these strategies on database performance, user experience, and overall system stability.

## Optimizing Database Performance through Maintenance

In conclusion, mastering index rebuilds and statistics updates is essential for beginners to optimize the performance and efficiency of MS SQL Server databases. By understanding the concepts, best practices, and techniques discussed in this guide, beginners can effectively

## Integrating MS SQL with Programming Languages: A Comprehensive Guide for Beginners

In the realm of database-driven applications, the integration of Microsoft SQL Server (MS SQL) with programming languages is essential for building dynamic, data-driven solutions. By connecting MS SQL with popular programming languages such as Python, C#, and others, developers can leverage the power of SQL queries, transactions, and data manipulation capabilities to create robust and efficient applications. For beginners in both database management and programming, understanding how to establish connections between MS SQL and programming languages opens up a world of possibilities for building sophisticated applications that interact seamlessly with databases. In this comprehensive guide, we will explore various methods and techniques for connecting MS SQL with programming languages, covering topics such as database connectivity libraries, SQL query execution, data retrieval and manipulation, and best practices for integration. By mastering the art of connecting MS SQL with programming languages, beginners can enhance their SQL skills and develop versatile applications that harness the full potential of relational databases.

# Chapter 1: Introduction to Database Connectivity

## 1.1 Understanding Database Connectivity:

- Define database connectivity and its importance in building applications that interact with MS SQL Server.
- Discuss the role of database connectivity libraries and drivers in establishing connections between programming languages and databases.

## 1.2 Overview of Database Drivers:

- Introduce common database drivers used for connecting MS SQL Server with programming languages, including ODBC, JDBC, ADO.NET, and OLE DB.
- Discuss the features, compatibility, and usage scenarios of each database driver.

## 1.3 Choosing the Right Database Driver:

- Provide guidelines for selecting the appropriate database driver based on programming language, platform compatibility, and performance requirements.
- Discuss factors such as ease of installation, community support, and feature support for making informed decisions.

# Chapter 2: Connecting MS SQL with Python

## 2.1 Introduction to PyODBC:

- Introduce PyODBC as a popular Python library for connecting to databases using the Open Database Connectivity (ODBC) interface.
- Discuss the features and capabilities of PyODBC for executing SQL queries, fetching results, and managing database connections.

## 2.2 Establishing Database Connections:

- Provide step-by-step instructions for establishing connections to MS SQL Server using PyODBC.
- Discuss connection string parameters, authentication methods, and error handling techniques.

## 2.3 Executing SQL Queries:

- Explain how to execute SQL queries against MS SQL Server using PyODBC.
- Discuss techniques for parameterized queries, batch execution, and retrieving result sets.

## 2.4 Data Retrieval and Manipulation:

- Explore methods for fetching and manipulating data retrieved from MS SQL Server using PyODBC.
- Discuss techniques for iterating over result sets, handling NULL values, and performing data transformations.

# Chapter 3: Connecting MS SQL with C#

## 3.1 ADO.NET Overview:

- Introduce ADO.NET as a data access technology for connecting applications to databases in the .NET framework.
- Discuss the architecture of ADO.NET and its components, including Connection, Command, DataReader, and DataSet.

## 3.2 Establishing SqlConnection:

- Provide code examples for establishing connections to MS SQL Server using the SqlConnection class in ADO.NET.
- Discuss connection string formatting, connection pooling, and error handling strategies.

## 3.3 Executing SQL Commands:

- Explain how to execute SQL commands against MS SQL Server using the SqlCommand class in ADO.NET.
- Discuss techniques for executing parameterized queries, stored procedures, and batch commands.

## 3.4 Retrieving and Manipulating Data:

- Explore methods for retrieving and manipulating data retrieved from MS SQL Server using SqlDataReader and DataSet in ADO.NET.
- Discuss techniques for data binding, data validation, and working with disconnected data.

# Chapter 4: Advanced Database Operations

## 4.1 Transactions and Error Handling:

- Discuss the importance of transactions and error handling in database operations.
- Explain how to manage transactions and handle exceptions when interacting with MS SQL Server from programming languages.

## 4.2 Stored Procedures and Prepared Statements:

- Introduce stored procedures and prepared statements as mechanisms for optimizing database performance and enhancing security.
- Discuss how to execute stored procedures and prepared statements from programming languages using parameterized commands.

## 4.3 Bulk Data Operations:

- Explore techniques for performing bulk data operations, such as bulk inserts, updates, and deletes, from programming languages.
- Discuss best practices for optimizing bulk data operations and minimizing performance overhead.

# Chapter 5: Best Practices for Database Integration

## 5.1 Connection Pooling:

- Discuss the benefits of connection pooling for improving application performance and scalability.
- Provide guidelines for configuring and managing connection pooling in programming languages when connecting to MS SQL Server.

## 5.2 Secure Database Access:

- Discuss best practices for securely accessing MS SQL Server from programming languages.
- Explore techniques for parameterized queries, input validation, and preventing SQL injection attacks.

## 5.3 Performance Optimization:

- Provide tips and techniques for optimizing database integration performance.
- Discuss strategies for optimizing query execution, minimizing round trips to the database, and reducing network latency.

# Chapter 6: Real-world Applications and Case Studies

## 6.1 Building Web Applications:

- Present real-world scenarios where MS SQL Server is integrated with programming languages to build web applications.
- Discuss the architecture, technologies used, and challenges faced in each scenario.

## 6.2 Data Analysis and Reporting:

- Present case studies of applications that leverage MS SQL Server for data analysis and reporting.
- Explore the integration of programming languages for generating dynamic reports, visualizations, and insights from database data.

# Mastering Database Integration with Programming Languages

In summary, connecting MS SQL Server to programming languages opens up a world of possibilities for building powerful applications and databases. By learning the concepts and best practices outlined in this guide, beginners can improve their SQL skills and create more efficient applications using the full power of relational databases. Whether creating websites, data analysis tools or publishing solutions, MS SQL Server's integration with programming languages allows developers to create powerful and efficient applications that will meet the needs of today's business world.

# Leveraging MS SQL in Web Development: A Beginner's Guide

In the world of web development, integration with Microsoft SQL Server (MS SQL) is important for creating dynamic and data-driven web applications. Whether you're building business applications with ASP.NET or flexible and scalable solutions with PHP, MS SQL is the foundation for efficient data storage and management. For those new to web development, understanding how to use MS SQL with popular web development tools is crucial to creating powerful and effective applications. In this guide, we'll examine the integration of MS SQL with web development like ASP.NET and PHP, including topics like database design, connections, queries, security, and best practices for operational excellence. By learning how to use MS SQL in web development, beginners can improve their SQL skills and create web applications that meet the needs of modern businesses, history and users.

# Chapter 1: Introduction to Web Development with MS SQL

## 1.1 Understanding Database-driven Web Development:

- Introduce the concept of database-driven web development and its significance in modern web applications.
- Discuss the role of MS SQL as a relational database management system (RDBMS) in storing, retrieving, and managing data for web applications.

## 1.2 Overview of Web Development Frameworks:

- Introduce popular web development frameworks such as ASP.NET and PHP.
- Discuss the features, benefits, and use cases of each framework in building dynamic web applications.

## 1.3 Importance of MS SQL in Web Development:

- Highlight the importance of MS SQL as a robust and scalable database solution for web development.
- Discuss the advantages of using MS SQL in conjunction with web development frameworks for data storage, retrieval, and manipulation.

# Chapter 2: Database Design for Web Applications

## 2.1 Database Design Principles:

- Introduce fundamental database design principles, including normalization, entity-relationship modeling, and schema design.
- Discuss the importance of designing database schemas that align with the requirements and functionality of web applications.

## 2.2 Designing Tables and Relationships:

- Explain how to design database tables and establish relationships between them for web applications.
- Discuss techniques for defining primary keys, foreign keys, and indexes to ensure data integrity and optimize query performance.

## 2.3 Data Modeling Considerations:

- Explore considerations for modeling data in MS SQL for web applications, including handling complex relationships, data types, and constraints.
- Discuss best practices for designing scalable and maintainable database schemas that support the evolving needs of web applications.

# Chapter 3: Connecting MS SQL with ASP.NET

### 3.1 Introduction to ASP.NET:

- Provide an overview of ASP.NET as a web development framework for building dynamic and interactive web applications.
- Discuss the architecture and components of ASP.NET, including Web Forms, MVC, and Razor Pages.

### 3.2 Establishing Database Connections:

- Explain how to establish connections to MS SQL Server from ASP.NET applications.
- Discuss techniques for configuring connection strings, managing database connections, and handling connection errors.

### 3.3 Data Access with ADO.NET:

- Introduce ADO.NET as the data access technology used in ASP.NET for interacting with databases.
- Discuss the use of ADO.NET classes such as SqlConnection, SqlCommand, and SqlDataReader for executing SQL queries and retrieving data from MS SQL Server.

### 3.4 Data Binding and Presentation:

- Explore methods for binding data retrieved from MS SQL Server to ASP.NET web controls for presentation.
- Discuss techniques for displaying data in grids, lists, forms, and other UI elements using data binding techniques in ASP.NET.

# Chapter 4: Connecting MS SQL with PHP

### 4.1 Introduction to PHP:

- Provide an overview of PHP as a server-side scripting language for web development.
- Discuss the features, syntax, and use cases of PHP in building dynamic and interactive web applications.

### .2 Using PDO for Database Connectivity:

- Explain how to establish connections to MS SQL Server from PHP applications using the PHP Data Objects (PDO) extension.
- Discuss the advantages of PDO for database connectivity and the steps involved in configuring database connections.

## 4.3 Executing SQL Queries:

- Discuss techniques for executing SQL queries against MS SQL Server from PHP applications using PDO.
- Provide examples of querying data, inserting records, updating data, and deleting records using prepared statements and parameterized queries.


# Chapter 5: Security Considerations in Web Development with MS SQL

## 5.1 SQL Injection Prevention:

- Discuss the risks of SQL injection attacks in web applications and the importance of mitigating these risks.
- Explore techniques for preventing SQL injection attacks, such as parameterized queries, input validation, and using parameterized stored procedures.

## 5.2 Authentication and Authorization:

- Discuss best practices for implementing authentication and authorization mechanisms in web applications.
- Explore techniques for validating user credentials, managing user sessions, and enforcing access controls to protect sensitive data stored in MS SQL Server.


# Chapter 6: Performance Optimization Techniques

## 6.1 Query Optimization:

- Discuss techniques for optimizing SQL queries executed against MS SQL Server for improved performance.
- Explore strategies such as indexing, query tuning, and execution plan analysis to optimize query performance in web applications.

## 6.2 Caching Strategies:

- Explain how caching can improve the performance of web applications by reducing database round trips and query execution times.
- Discuss techniques for implementing caching mechanisms in web applications to store frequently accessed data and improve response times.

## 6.3 Connection Pooling:

- Discuss the benefits of connection pooling for improving the scalability and performance of web applications.

- Provide guidance on configuring connection pooling settings in ASP.NET and PHP applications to efficiently manage database connections.

# Chapter 7: Real-world Applications and Case Studies

## 7.1 Building E-commerce Platforms:

- Present real-world examples of e-commerce platforms built using MS SQL and web development frameworks such as ASP.NET and PHP.
- Discuss the architecture, features, and scalability considerations of each platform.

## 7.2 Developing Content Management Systems (CMS):

- Showcase case studies of content management systems developed with MS SQL and web development frameworks.
- Explore the customization options, extensibility, and performance optimizations implemented in each CMS.

# Harnessing the Power of MS SQL in Web Development

Harness the power of MS SQL in Web Development In conclusion, using MS SQL Server along with web development such as ASP.NET and PHP allows developers to create competitive, scalable and secure web applications. By learning how to integrate MS SQL with web development, beginners can improve their SQL skills and create versatile applications to meet the changing needs of users and businesses in the digital age.

# Integrating MS SQL in Business Intelligence Solutions: A Beginner's Guide

In today's business environment, data plays an important role in making effective and profitable decisions. Business intelligence (BI) solutions enable organizations to transform raw data into insights that enable stakeholders to make informed decisions. Microsoft SQL Server (MS SQL) provides a solid foundation for storing and managing data, making it an essential part of many BI architectures. For beginners who want to improve their MS SQL skills and dive deeper into the world of business intelligence, it is important to understand how to integrate MS SQL into BI solutions. In this guide, we will examine the integration of MS SQL with popular BI tools such as Power BI, including topics such as data models, ETL (Extract, Transform, Load) methods process, report generation, and data visualization. By mastering the integration of MS SQL into business intelligence solutions, startups can unlock the full potential of their data and drive business growth with informed decisions.

## Chapter 1: Introduction to Business Intelligence and MS SQL

1.1 Understanding Business Intelligence:

  - Define Business Intelligence (BI) and its role in transforming data into actionable insights.
  - Discuss the benefits of BI for organizations, including improved decision-making, enhanced operational efficiency, and competitive advantage.

1.2 Overview of MS SQL Server:

  - Introduce Microsoft SQL Server (MS SQL) as a leading relational database management system (RDBMS).
  - Discuss the features and capabilities of MS SQL for storing, managing, and analyzing data.

1.3 Importance of MS SQL in Business Intelligence:

  - Highlight the role of MS SQL as a foundational component of business intelligence solutions.
  - Discuss how MS SQL enables organizations to centralize data, perform complex analytics, and drive BI initiatives.

# Chapter 2: Data Modeling and Preparation with MS SQL

## 2.1 Data Modeling Fundamentals:

- Introduce the concept of data modeling and its importance in BI solutions.
- Discuss common data modeling techniques, including dimensional modeling and star schemas.

## 2.2 Designing Data Models in MS SQL:

- Explore techniques for designing data models in MS SQL Server for business intelligence applications.
- Discuss considerations such as entity-relationship diagrams, normalization, and denormalization.

## 2.3 Data Preparation and ETL Processes:

- Explain the Extract, Transform, Load (ETL) process and its role in preparing data for analysis in BI solutions.
- Discuss how to implement ETL processes using tools such as SQL Server Integration Services (SSIS) for data extraction, transformation, and loading.

# Chapter 3: Integrating MS SQL with Power BI

## 3.1 Introduction to Power BI:

- Provide an overview of Power BI as a leading self-service BI tool developed by Microsoft.
- Discuss the features and capabilities of Power BI for data visualization, analysis, and reporting.

## 3.2 Connecting to MS SQL Server:

- Explain how to connect Power BI to MS SQL Server for accessing data stored in MS SQL databases.
- Discuss different connection methods, including direct connections, import mode, and DirectQuery mode.

## 3.3 Data Import and Transformation:

- Explore techniques for importing and transforming data from MS SQL Server into Power BI.
- Discuss Power Query as a powerful tool for data transformation and cleansing within Power BI.

# Chapter 4: Building Data Models and Relationships

## 4.1 Creating Data Models in Power BI:

- Explain how to design data models within Power BI using the Power BI Desktop application.
- Discuss concepts such as tables, relationships, calculated columns, and measures.

## 4.2 Establishing Relationships:

- Discuss the importance of establishing relationships between tables in Power BI data models.
- Explore techniques for defining and managing relationships to ensure accurate data analysis and visualization.

# Chapter 5: Creating Reports and Dashboards

## 5.1 Designing Reports in Power BI:

- Explore the capabilities of Power BI for designing interactive and visually appealing reports.
- Discuss techniques for creating tables, charts, maps, and other visualizations to convey insights effectively.

## 5.2 Building Dashboards:

- Explain how to assemble reports and visualizations into interactive dashboards within Power BI.
- Discuss best practices for dashboard design, layout, and interactivity to facilitate data exploration and decision-making.

# Chapter 6: Advanced Analytics and Insights

## 6.1 Advanced Analytics Features:

- Explore advanced analytics features available in Power BI for predictive modeling, statistical analysis, and machine learning.
- Discuss techniques for leveraging these features to uncover insights and trends in data stored in MS SQL Server.

## 6.2 Data Exploration and Discovery:

- Discuss techniques for exploring and analyzing data within Power BI to uncover hidden patterns, trends, and outliers.

- Explore features such as drill-down, cross-filtering, and natural language querying for data exploration.

# Chapter 7: Collaboration and Distribution

## 7.1 Collaborative BI:

- Discuss the importance of collaborative BI for sharing insights and fostering data-driven decision-making across organizations.
- Explore features in Power BI for collaboration, including sharing, commenting, and collaboration workspaces.

## 7.2 Distribution and Deployment:

- Explain how to deploy and distribute Power BI reports and dashboards to end-users within and outside the organization.
- Discuss options for embedding Power BI content into web applications, portals, and other platforms.

# Chapter 8: Security and Governance

## 8.1 Data Security:

- Discuss best practices for ensuring data security and privacy within Power BI and MS SQL Server.
- Explore features such as row-level security, encryption, and data masking for protecting sensitive information.

## 8.2 Governance and Compliance:

- Explain the importance of governance and compliance in BI solutions, particularly in regulated industries.
- Discuss techniques for implementing governance policies, auditing data access, and ensuring regulatory compliance.

# Chapter 9: Performance Optimization

## 9.1 Query Performance Optimization:

- Discuss techniques for optimizing query performance in MS SQL Server for BI workloads.
- Explore indexing strategies, query tuning, and performance monitoring techniques.

## 9.2 Power BI Performance Optimization:

- Provide tips and best practices for optimizing performance in Power BI reports and dashboards.
- Discuss techniques for optimizing data refresh schedules, reducing report rendering times, and improving overall responsiveness.

# Chapter 10: Real-world Applications and Case Studies

## 10.1 Business Intelligence Case Studies:

- Present real-world examples of organizations using MS SQL Server and Power BI to drive business intelligence initiatives.
- Discuss the challenges faced, solutions implemented, and outcomes achieved in each case study.

# Unlocking the Power of BI with MS SQL

In summary, incorporating MS SQL Server into business intelligence solutions enables organizations to leverage data and gain insights that drive business growth and innovation. By learning how to integrate MS SQL with tools like Power BI, beginners can improve their BI skills and contribute to data-driven decision-making in their organizations. With the knowledge and ideas provided in this guide, beginners can begin their journey to becoming a BI expert ready to face the challenges of today's data-driven world.